Everybody's A Winner

Everybody's
A
Winner

A Kid's Guide to New Sports and Fitness

Written by Tom Schneider

Illustrated by Richard Wilson and Tom Schneider

LITTLE, BROWN AND COMPANY
Boston   Toronto

This Brown Paper School book was edited and prepared for publication at The Yolla Bolly Press, Covelo, California, between November 1975 and May 1976. The series is under the supervision of James and Carolyn Robertson. Production staff members are: Colleen Carter, Sharon Miley, and Gene Floyd.

First edition. Published simultaneously in Canada by Little, Brown & Company (Canada) Limited.
Printed in the United States of America.

T 10/76

Library of Congress Cataloging in Publication Data

Schneider, Tom.
    Everybody's a winner.

    (The brown paper school)
    SUMMARY: A guide to all-new, non-competitive sports and games which don't need special equipment and which anyone can play. Includes such games as New Frisbee, Infinity Volleyball, and information on fitness and yoga.
    1. Sports for children — Juvenile literature. 2. Physical fitness — Juvenile literature. [1. Sports. 2. Physical fitness] I. Title.
GV709.2.S36   613.7'042   76-14404
ISBN 0-316-77398-0
ISBN 0-316-77399-9 pbk.

About this book

We all change our minds now and then and nobody much
notices. But when *lots* of people change their minds about
the *same* thing at more or less the same time, *everybody*
notices. Right now a lot of people are changing their minds
about playing sports. There are new games. There are new
ways to play the old ones. And maybe most important, there
are new ways to think about winning and losing. It turns out
that winning might have more to do with what you learn and
how you feel than it does with ribbons or prizes or being best.
It turns out that maybe everybody is a winner — or could be.
This book tells about new games and new ideas and what they
might mean to *you*.

What's in this Book

Everybody's A Winner

Imagine for a moment

the year 2000.

What will sports be like? What new games will be played?

Let's suppose it's a late summer afternoon, on September 22, 2000.
A group of about a thousand families is gathering for a day of picnic
lunches, new sports, and games. They're celebrating the autumnal
equinox, the day summer ends, and fall begins.

But today, summer still reigns in this wild valley. The sun is hot, and
bare feet stir up pungent, spicy odors from the dry grasses.

People of all sizes and ages are streaming into the valley. They carry
baskets of food, blankets, brightly colored kites, balls, and balloons.
Some people ride bicycles — but most walk the quarter-mile from the
end of the electric train line.

Years ago, in the 1970s, a housing development was planned for this
valley. But the people of the nearby city said, "No. We need more open
spaces. Leave this unbuilt."

So the land was protected, and it grew wild. It became the place where
festivals were held; where city people could be close to the land; where
they could celebrate nature, and learn to be a part of it.

11

Activity is increasing in the valley now. Lunches have been quickly consumed by some, and the first games are getting underway. Elsewhere, people lie in the grass, fly kites, and play music.

At the end of the valley, a giant ship's hawser has been stretched across the creek. A game of Le Mans Tug-O-War is about to begin.

Then there is Parachute Madness. Fifty people are trying to move together and keep the parachute aloft.

A NEW GAMES FESTIVAL

Over on the dirt road, a Bicycle Gymkhana is being organized. Kids and adults are starting through the course in a wild array of two-wheeled machines.

Earth Ball, a giant, heavier-than-air balloon, is being set in motion in the meadow, and hundreds of people are racing to join the game.

New Frisbee, Infinity Volleyball, Yogi Tag. Games start up and end. There is no Grand Plan. People move toward centers of activity, then move away to rest. Everybody plays. No one is hurt.

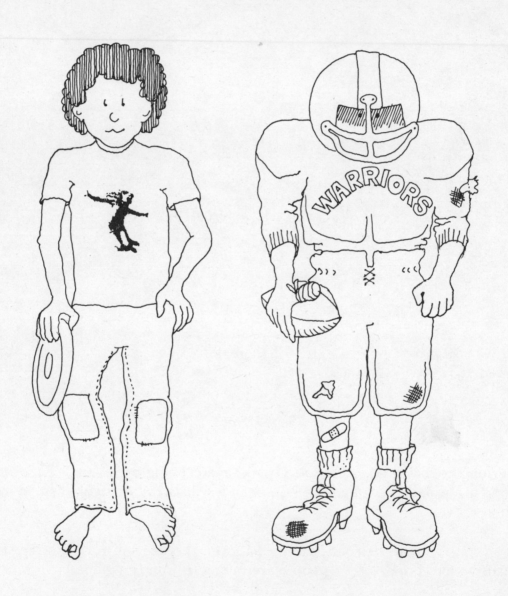

Equipment needed
for a New Games Festival

Equipment needed
for a Superbowl Game

There's a lot of difference between a New Games Festival and a professional sports "Spectacular."

"Winning is everything!" said a famous football coach. "Winning means nothing," say New Games players. "It's how you play that counts." New Games are usually *non-competitive*. They are played for the joy of playing.

In pro football, you play to win. Almost all professional sporting events are designed around winning and losing.

Competition, seasoned with money, is what leads to Super Athletes. When the stakes are so high, no team can afford to gamble on any but the biggest, strongest, fastest, hardest-hitting players.

But what about all the rest of us? Are we stuck on the sidelines, unequipped spectators?

New Games offer a way we can all play. And that's what this book is about.

1

New Games – New Rules

Can you imagine playing tag with a blindfold on? Or trying to enter a spinning jump rope with your feet tied together? Or swimming while wearing an overcoat and galoshes? With those handicaps, the games become ridiculous, maybe impossible. Yet is this really any different from imagining you or me playing basketball against six-foot eleven-inch Bill Walton? Or football against 285-pound Rosie Grier?

Organized, competitive sports are for specialists. In football, if you're not big, you'd better be very fast. In baseball, if you can't bat at least .200, you'd better turn in your spikes.

Now suppose you could change one rule in the game. Could you change basketball so that someone four feet tall could play and have an equal chance with someone seven feet tall?

You could lower the baskets. You could make everyone over five feet play with only one hand. What else?

Rules make the game. And, over a period of time, the game makes the players.

How can this be? Well, basketball was not invented because there were a lot of well-coordinated, tall people around. It started out as a game for idle kids to play, indoors, in the lull between football and baseball seasons.

But basketball became an almost instant hit. Success brought promoters and big money to the game. The search for professional players began. It wasn't long before someone noticed that tall players have an advantage in this game. And getting from there to present-day teams of giants was just a process of selection. The rules made the game and the game selected the players.

In New Games all this gets turned around. In contrast to sports that tend to single out the best specialists, New Games are purposely designed so that everyone can play. Some New Games involve contests between players, but the real fun comes in playing the games, not in winning them.

Designing a New Game

The invention of one game, New Frisbee, has been carefully documented. By following its design and playing it, you might learn something about designing any new game.

Two of the inventors of New Frisbee are George Leonard and Hugh Knowlton. As pilots in World War II they became interested in the idea of maximum performance. It worked like this: Even if they had a 10,000-foot runway, they would always try to touch down in the first 50 feet. If the rules allowed them to fly within 200 feet, plus or minus, of a certain altitude, they would make a supreme effort to fly the *exact* altitude. They made a kind of game out of trying for the best possible performance. Not because they wanted to show off, or because of rules and regulations, but just for the pure pleasure of being very good at something.

New Frisbee developed from this spirit of excellence. And yet in New Frisbee, excellence is meant in the broadest possible sense.

Even a physical handicap need not keep you from playing the game. New Frisbee is designed so that you score by doing your best. Not someone else's best, *your* best.

In New Frisbee, a person with one leg can play as an equal with a champion runner. Here's how it works:

Rules for New Frisbee

The game is played with a regulation-size Frisbee. Before beginning to play, both players state with which hand they will throw and catch. They may throw with one hand and catch with the other, or throw and catch with the same hand. But they must stick to their stated choice throughout the game.

Players stand 15 or 20 yards apart and take turns throwing. The thrower launches the Frisbee in any direction. The catcher makes an all-out effort to catch it.

If the catcher touches the Frisbee, then drops it, the catcher gives the thrower two points. The catcher must also award two points if the Frisbee is caught with the wrong hand, or if it's caught by cradling against the body.

If the Frisbee should tilt more than 45 degrees from the horizontal at any time during its flight, the catcher may call "Forty-five!" The catcher can then take one point without attempting to make a catch.

If the catcher cannot possibly reach the Frisbee at any time during its flight, this is a thrower's error and the catcher takes one point.

If the Frisbee is thrown in such a way that the catcher *could* possibly catch it, but fails to make an all-out effort, or misjudges the Frisbee's flight, the catcher gives one point to the thrower.

If the catcher is in danger of running into an obstacle, the catcher or thrower should call "Obstacle!" The point is then re-played.

Note that the catcher calls all points. Upon hearing a call the thrower must not make an outcry or any gesture of disapproval.

There are no judges or referees in this game. The players themselves determine how points will be awarded.

Scoring

A casual game is played to 11 points. Players change sides when one reaches 6 points.

A match game is 21 points. Players change sides when one reaches 11 points.

The scoring system makes New Frisbee a competitive game. You do play to win, because putting out your best effort and playing to win are the same kind of thing.

The difference between New Frisbee and other competitive games is that you adjust the game to each player's level of skill. It's as if you were playing against Bill Walton and his basket was nine feet high, but yours was at five feet.

And New Frisbee does not encourage you to be a boastful winner. The method of scoring makes you constantly appreciate the other player's skill, as well as your own. When the game is over, no matter who has the most points, both players have "won." Both have played hard and fair, the best they know how.

A Test for New Games

1. Can everybody play?
2. Can anybody win?
3. Will anyone get hurt?
4. Is it fun?

Care to try the New Games Test on pro football?

Football is probably the most competitive of all professional sports. Not only is big money at stake. Players also risk torn ligaments, broken bones, and other injuries that may last a lifetime.

But it's not just on the football field that winning takes such a toll. Destructive competition finds its way into every part of our lives. It even enters into how we feel about our bodies. "Is my body better looking than . . . or stronger than . . . or taller than someone else's body?" These are competitive questions. When you ask them, you want to know how you compare to someone other than yourself.

New Games don't require that you have a new body. The one you're in will do just fine. All you need to do is to find out what you have got, and make the best use of it. That's what the next few chapters are about.

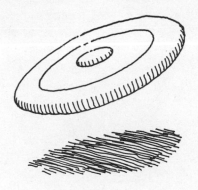

We'll Call It Basketball

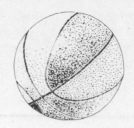

THERE is no mystery about the origin of basketball. It was invented in 1891 by Dr. James A. Naismith, a YMCA instructor in Springfield, Massachusetts. Dr. Naismith's own account of his process of invention makes interesting reading for anyone interested in New Games:

"**I** FIRST tried to modify some of the existing games so they would meet the requirements, but failed to make any game suitable for indoor work. I then left out the idea of any individual game and began to think of the fundamental principles of all games. I discovered that in all team games some kind of ball was used.

"**T**HE next step was to appreciate the fact that football was rough because of tackling. Tackling was necessary because the offense ran with the ball. Accordingly, if the offense did not have an opportunity to run with the ball, there would be no need for tackling, and we would thus eliminate roughness.

"**T**HIS is the fundamental principle of basketball.

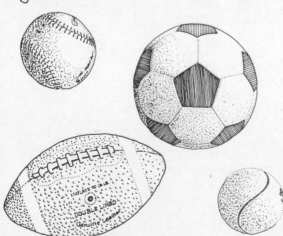

No touching.

"THE next step was to secure some kind of a goal through which the ball could be passed. I decided that by making the goal horizontal the ball would have to be thrown in a curve, minimizing the severe driving of a ball. In order to avoid having the defense congregate around the goal it was placed above their heads, so that once the ball left the individual's hands, it was not likely to be interfered with.

"THEN rules were made to eliminate roughness such as shouldering, pushing, kicking, etc. The ball was to be handled with the hands only. It could not be drawn into the body and thus encourage roughness.

Dr. James A. Naismith

"THE manner of putting the ball into play was then considered. Two individuals were selected and took their stations in the middle of the floor. The ball was thrown up so as to land between them, giving as nearly equal chance as possible.

"THE nearest approach to the ball needed was the soccer ball, so we selected that.

"TO make the goals we used a couple of old peach baskets, hanging one at each end of the gym.

"FROM this basketball developed."

THE peach baskets are gone, and the game now has its own special ball, but many of the basic rules that Dr. Naismith laid down in 1891 are still in effect today.

2
Anybody Home in There?

Have you ever come home from a football game — one where you wore a helmet and shoulder pads and a jersey, and you really worked up a sweat? Wasn't it great when you finally got all that stuff off? The air could get to your skin, and you felt as if you could breathe again, right?

Or, maybe you live where there's snow that has to be shoveled. You wrap all up — putting on your scarf, knit cap, mittens, boots — and you work really hard. When you come in and get all those heavy clothes off, don't you feel good — kind of loose and free?

If you saw people walking around in football gear all the time, or bundled up in snow clothes all year round, you'd probably think they were crazy. Yet some psychologists think that we're *all* wearing "uniforms," heavy, padded, protective clothing, much of the time. Only it can't be seen.

Psychologists call this "protective armor."

Imagine people like the Knights of the Round Table, wearing heavy, clanking, metal armor. Now imagine it's there on all of us, but it's invisible.

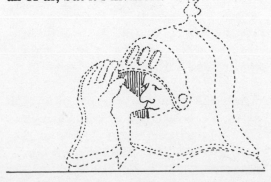

Do *you* wear armor? Most everybody does at some time or other. Have you ever pretended to be pleased and happy when inside you felt mad enough to burst? Have you ever pretended to be sick, just so you wouldn't have to do something, even though you felt fine?

You can hide your true feelings, pretend to *be* other than you *are*, by putting on your protective armor. It's kind of like wearing a Halloween mask.

Sometimes it's for someone else's sake that you hide your feelings. For instance, you pretend you like your birthday sweater (even though you just *hate* that color) so you won't make your parents feel bad.

But too much armor is hard on you. Because if you're pretending and fooling other people a *lot* of the time, you may also be fooling yourself. That is, you may be fooling your mind. Your body always knows how it really feels, and it doesn't like not being able to show it.

When your body has this kind of mental armor on, it feels like you do when you have a lot of tight, heavy clothes on. It feels stiff and rigid, and it doesn't move very well.

Anybody Home?

Here's an exercise for getting in touch with your body. It will tell you if your body is agreeing with, or arguing with, your mind. The exercise has several parts, and you needn't do them all at once. Take your time.

Almost everybody has a picture in their mind of how they look. This can also be a kind of armor. "I'm fat. I'm skinny. I'm short. I'm tall." These are some of the pictures that people usually have of themselves. What is yours?

Try to bring that picture to life. Find a place where you can be alone for a while in front of a large mirror. Take off some or all of your clothes.

Look at the image of your body in the mirror. Do you like it? If you do, congratulations! Your body is unique and special. There's none other like it.

If you *don't* like your body, you may be blinded by your mental picture. You may be worried about how you *wish* your body could be:

IF YOU WISH: Your muscles were bigger.

TRY THIS: Flex your arms, be a muscle man. Pretend your muscles are twice as big — 4 times as big — 10 times as big!

AND THEN THINK ABOUT THIS: Extra muscle means extra weight. That can slow you down. Look at basketball players: They are fast but not especially muscular.

IF YOU WISH: You were taller.

TRY THIS: Start growing in your mind. Pretend you are a foot taller — 2 feet taller — 6 feet taller! Stand on a box, see how you look.

AND THEN THINK ABOUT THIS: Really tall people often dream about being short. They have all kinds of problems getting into cars; under doorways; finding clothes that fit. (They also don't make good jockeys.)

IF YOU WISH: You were not so fat.

TRY THIS: Imagine you just lost 10 pounds — 20 pounds — 60 pounds! How do you look — thin?

AND THEN THINK ABOUT THIS: Did you know that almost all skinny people would like to be fatter? By the way, fat makes you float. You could be good at swimming.

IF YOU WISH: You were not so skinny.

TRY THIS: Imagine you just gained 10 pounds — 20 pounds — 60 pounds! How do you look — fat?

AND THEN THINK ABOUT THIS: Did you know that almost everybody else worries about being too fat? They envy you. Thin people are usually the best runners and jumpers. Can you figure out why?

Here's another way to get around those wishes:

Three Fables

1. Imagine that you are the first person on earth. You are perfect, and you will be the model for all the people who come after you. You are the standard by which others will be judged.

3. You are the boss of all the newspapers, magazines, and TV. You decide that every picture in every advertisement or story must show someone who looks like you. Pretty soon, because they saw it on TV, or in a magazine, everybody thinks that's what they should look like. They all want to look like you!

These exercises should help you realize that there is no "ideal body."

People's ideas about "good looks" are always changing. Two hundred years ago, women were thought to be very beautiful when they were very round — what today we would call fat. Now, to be in fashion, some women try to almost starve.

2. Now make yourself a king. All your loyal subjects love you and want to be just like you. They all go on diets, or try to gain weight. They wear stacked heels, or they slouch. Every day they try to look more like you.

Times do change.

Mirror, Mirror on the Wall

While you're in front of that full-length mirror, try these other exercises to get a more complete picture of the real you.

A second mirror, one you can hold and move around, will come in handy.

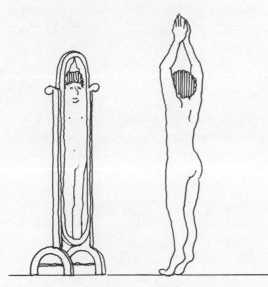

Stretch your arms over your head and stand on your tiptoes. Look at your body in this position.

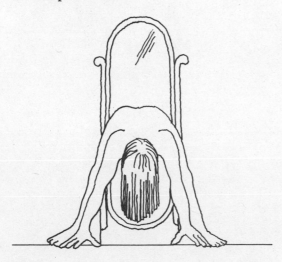

Now stand with your back to the mirror, legs about a foot apart. Bend and try to touch the floor with your fingertips. While you're down there, look back at your image in the mirror.

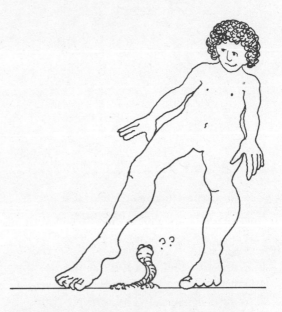

Put the small mirror on the floor and stand over it. Look down and see yourself from a worm's point of view.

Now hold the mirror directly over your head. Look up and see yourself as birds do.

Use the hand mirror and the full-length mirror to see the back and sides of your body.

Lift up your feet and look at the bottoms.

Study your hands in the mirror. Move the fingers one by one.

Move in front of the mirror. Pretend that you are swimming in the air, or hitting an imaginary line drive to center field, or making a game-winning serve at Wimbledon, or . . . ? Watch your body as it moves.

Your body is a prize possession. It is the only one like it in the world. Tell your body that you are proud of it (even if there are a few things you would like to change).

Walt "Clyde" Frazier's Mirror Routine

After taping his ankles and carefully putting on a crisp, fresh uniform, Walt Frazier spends about ten minutes in front of a mirror. He straightens his hair and pats down his sideburns. He mashes down his mustache — so the little hairs won't tickle his nose. Then he says to himself something like this: "Yeah, Clyde, you've got it!"

Walt feels that this little routine gives him the boost he needs to go out and play his best.

3

The Shape I'm In

Imagine for a moment that you are an invader from outer space. You have taken on the body of an earthling so that you may travel about undetected. Your mission is to find out what it's like to live as a human being.

The first part of your task will be to get to know your new body and find out what it can do.

Test No. 1

THE AMAZING
BODY TYPES DISCOVERY

"The *ectomorph* has a lightweight skeleton and very little fat. True ectomorphs are thin all of their lives.

"Understand that humans come in three forms, or shapes:

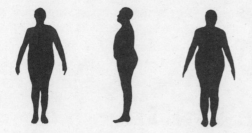

"The *endomorph* has a heavy skeleton and large amounts of rounded flesh. Even if they diet, endomorphs will still be rounder and fleshier than ectomorphs.

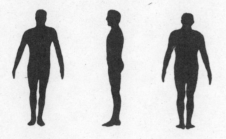

"The *mesomorph* has a medium-weight skeleton and very little fat, but may weigh as much as an endomorph of equal height because of well-developed muscles.

"No human fits any one of these types exactly. But everyone tends to be one of these three basic shapes."

To do this test, you'll need a slide projector (or a movie projector). If you can't borrow a projector, try to get a light bulb with a built-in reflector.

(An *unfrosted* bulb will also work.)

You'll also need two unfolded pages of a newspaper. (The want-ad section is best.)

Tape the two sheets of newspaper together like this:

Tape the newspapers to a wall or door, just above the floor. Set up the projector, or bulb, so that it covers the paper with white light.

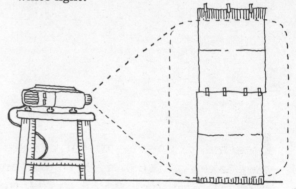

Now stand, your back to the light, about eight inches from the wall. Hold your arms out away from your body and place your feet about six inches apart. Ask a friend to trace around your shadow on the newspaper using a crayon or marking pen.

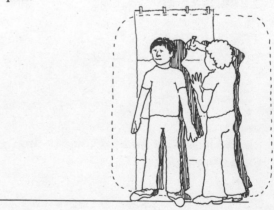

Now turn sideways (still eight inches from the wall) and have your friend trace the shadow you make this way. This time, keep your arms at your sides and your feet together. Ask your friend to use a different-colored marker for this shadow. Then you'll be able to draw right over the other outline and still tell them apart.

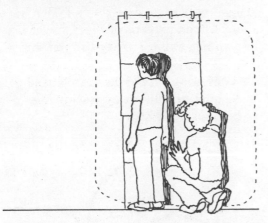

While the light is set up, you might want to trace your friend's front and side shadows on a different piece of newspaper. Then you can put the projector, or lamp, away.

Now get a ruler, or better yet, a tape measure. Lay your shadow tracings on the floor so that you can measure them easily.

First measure the height of each shadow. It may be somewhat greater than your actual height. That's okay. You're just going to see how the measurements compare; the actual numbers are not important.

Measure the shoulders, waist, hips, and thighs of the wide, front-view shadow. (The thigh measurement is taken at the widest part.) Write all these measurements on the newspaper.

Now measure the chest (at the widest part), the waist, and the calf (widest part), on the profile shadow outline. Make a note of these, too.

Add all of the numbers together like this:

Front view:	shoulders	39 cm.
	waist	22
	hips	20
	thigh	10
Side view:	chest	23
	waist	24
	calf	13
	Total	151 cm.

And then divide that total by the height:

$$\left(\text{Total}\right) 151\,\text{cm.} \div \left(\substack{\text{Shadow} \\ \text{Height}}\right) 115\,\text{cm.} = \boxed{1.31}$$

Compare the number you get with this chart to get an idea of your body type:

Endomorph	2.00
(Endo - Meso)	1.65
Mesomorph	1.35
(Ecto - Meso)	1.20
Ectomorph	1.00

Here's the importance of this discovery: No one can change their body type. An ectomorph will always be an ectomorph. Even if they eat like horses, they probably won't get fat. Likewise, an endomorph and a mesomorph are not likely to become skinny.

Body type is something humans are born with. It comes from one or both parents. (If your body is a very different type from your parents, perhaps you got your shape from your grandparents.)

Body type is like hair color. It's one of those things that make each human unique and different from the rest.

Test No. 2

HUMANS ARE FLESHAPODS

You've probably noticed by now that the males on this planet are different from the females. One way to tell this is to measure the amount of fat they have. (There must be an easier way.) Men have about fifteen percent of their weight in fat; women about twenty-five percent.

Test the body you're in. You'll need to make a set of calipers by tracing this pattern on thin paper:

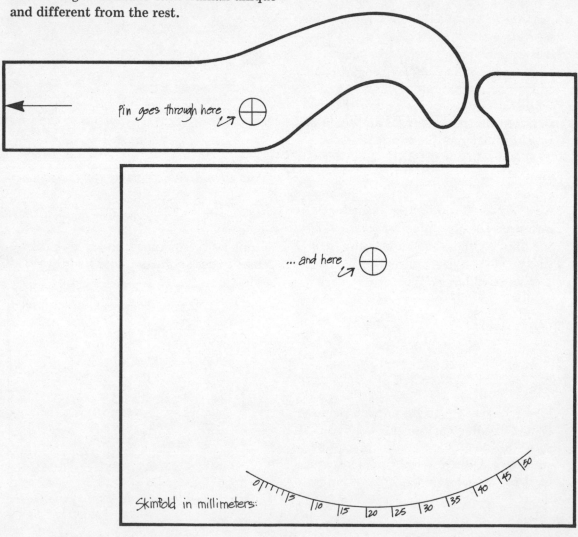

Pin goes through here

... and here

Skinfold in millimeters:

Mount the tracing on a piece of cardboard and then cut around the outline. A simple pivot can be made by sticking a straight pin through both hole marks and into an eraser.

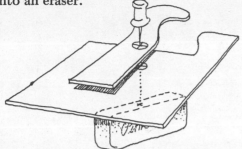

You'll need a friend to help you do the measuring.

First measurement (triceps): **Stand relax-ed, arms at your sides.** First your friend squeezes the loose flesh at the back of your arm, opposite your biceps, about halfway between your elbow and your shoulder.

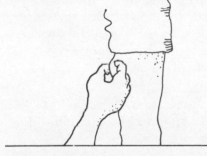

Your friend must hold the fold of flesh between thumb and forefinger, and measure it with the calipers. The calipers should make a slight dent in the flesh.

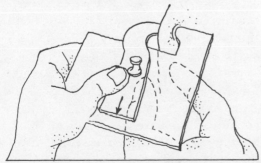

Holding the flesh and working the calipers can be a bit tricky. So it's best to take three measurements and then figure the average of all of them.

Example:

1st try	12
2nd try	8
3rd try	10
Total:	30

Divided by three tries = 10 (average)

Second measurement (biceps): **Again,** let your arms hang loosely at your sides. Measure a skin fold at the front of your arm, directly opposite from where you took the first measurement.

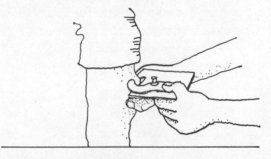

Find the average of three tries.

Third measurement (hip): **Pull your shirt out and bend from the waist, sideways:**

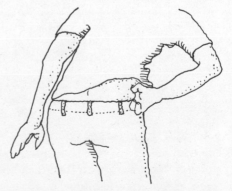

Have your friend measure the fold of flesh that forms parallel to your belt, just above your waist.

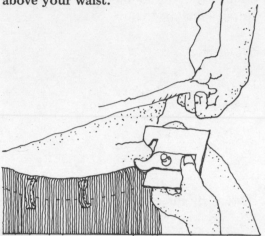

Total mm.	% Fat	mm.	%
15	5	75	25
20	9	80	24
25	11	75	25
30	13	80	26
35	15	90	27
40	17	100	28
45	18	110	29
50	20	120	30
55	21	130	31
60	22	140	32
65	23	150	33
70	24	160	34

Again, make several tries, find the average, and make a note of it.

Fourth measurement (upper back): Have your friend measure a skin fold just below your shoulder blade. The fold should be at a 45 degree angle to the vertical. Again, take three measurements and average them.

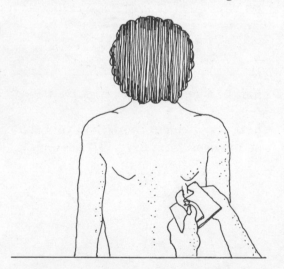

Finally, add the averages you got in each of the four tests. Locate that number on this chart. Next to it you'll find the percentage of fat in your body.

The sneaky thing about fat is that it doesn't weigh very much — only about a third as much as muscle. That's why you can't take those "ideal" weight/height charts too seriously. You can have an unhealthy high percentage of fat and still not be overweight by the charts. Someone with a high percentage of heavy muscle might be overweight by the charts, yet have a very low percentage of fat and be in excellent shape.

There are some other things that can make this "ideal" body weight an impossible goal. Bones, for example.

Human bones can add up to as much as 25 percent of total body weight. Just for comparison, a full-grown pelican may weigh in at 20 pounds. Of that, only 12 ounces, or less than 5 percent will be the bird's bones. Humans, with their heavy skeletons, were clearly never meant to fly!

The weight of your bones changes as you grow. Before you were born, your bones amounted to about 18 percent of your body weight. When you are fully grown they may be 25 percent or more.

Weighty Problems

Some people get very hung-up about weighing a certain amount, no more, no less. Actually, everybody's weight is constantly changing. You can prove this with a few simple experiments:

Weigh yourself when you get up and just before you go to bed. Do you shrink during the day?

Does eating make a difference in your weight? Weigh yourself before and after a "heavy" meal.

"By now you should realize that humans come in a great variety of shapes, sizes, and weights. We have never seen two of them exactly alike. Clearly, they are experimenting, trying to come up with a perfect model. From the looks of things they may never succeed in this."

39

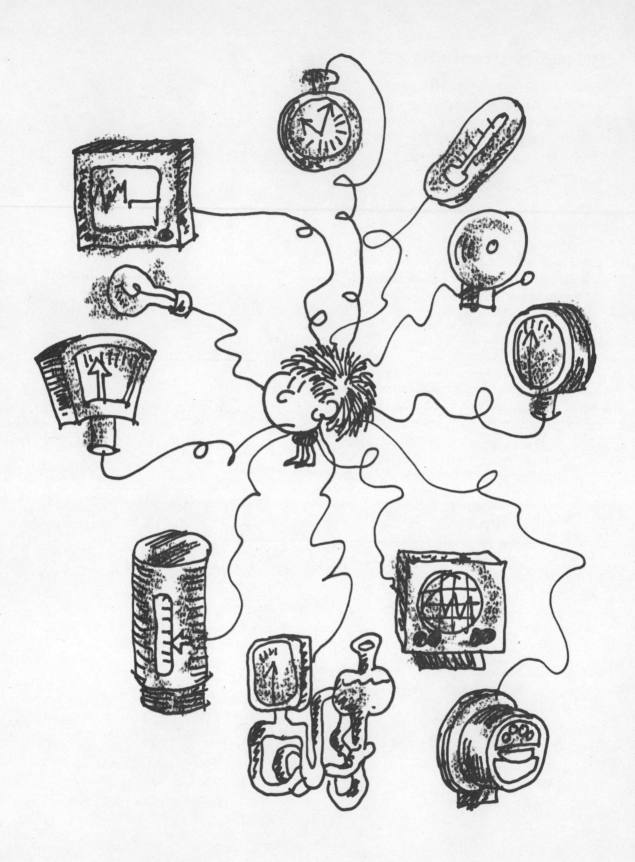

4

What'll She Do?

(A Road Test for Your Body)

If you were about to buy a new car, you'd probably want to drive it first. You might even read some of the many car magazines and study the test reports. Car buyers try to answer the question "What'll she do?" But do they ever ask the same question about their own bodies? Do you?

It seems only fair that people give as much time to studying their main means of transportation — their bodies — as they do to their secondary means of movement — their cars.

Yet car enthusiasts will get most excited about miles-per-gallon, acceleration rates, and the like, while their bodies are running out of gas.

You, on the other hand, can put first things first. Borrowing a few tips from the car nuts, you can give your own body a "road test."

Finding out how your body performs is important for two reasons:

1. A *complete* performance test usually gives you some good news about your body. Even if you could be better in some of the tests, in many areas you'll surprise yourself with success. And you should know what's *right* as well as what's not right with your body.

2. If you plan to improve your body's performance, you need some baseline measurements to start with — something to compare your progress with. These tests give you just that.

A complete performance test checks you in many areas:

endurance (heart and lungs)

agility

balance

flexibility

speed

power

strength

relaxation

On the following pages, you'll find at least one test for each of these abilities. To help keep a record of how you do, make a performance test scoresheet like this:

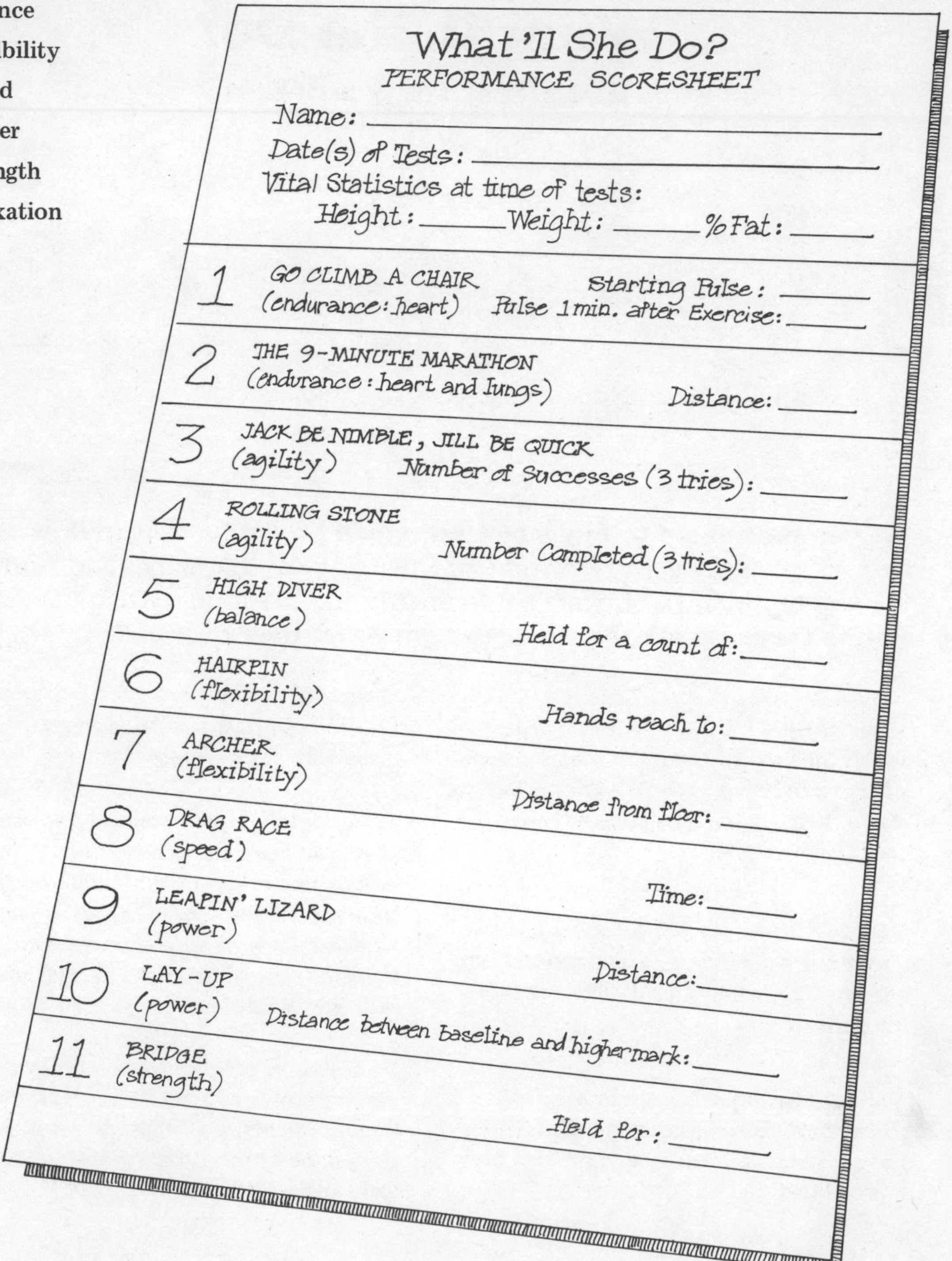

What'll She Do?
PERFORMANCE SCORESHEET

Name: _____

Date(s) of Tests: _____

Vital Statistics at time of tests:

Height: _____ Weight: _____ % Fat: _____

1 GO CLIMB A CHAIR   Starting Pulse: _____
(endurance: heart)   Pulse 1 min. after Exercise: _____

2 THE 9-MINUTE MARATHON
(endurance: heart and lungs)   Distance: _____

3 JACK BE NIMBLE, JILL BE QUICK
(agility)   Number of Successes (3 tries): _____

4 ROLLING STONE
(agility)   Number Completed (3 tries): _____

5 HIGH DIVER
(balance)   Held for a count of: _____

6 HAIRPIN
(flexibility)   Hands reach to: _____

7 ARCHER
(flexibility)   Distance from floor: _____

8 DRAG RACE
(speed)   Time: _____

9 LEAPIN' LIZARD
(power)   Distance: _____

10 LAY-UP
(power)   Distance between baseline and higher mark: _____

11 BRIDGE
(strength)   Held for: _____

Go Climb a Chair

(A test of endurance: heart rate.)

Endurance is your body's ability to work or play hard for a long time. This ability depends partly on how well your heart can pump oxygen-rich blood from your lungs to all parts of your body. Taking your pulse (heartbeats per minute) before and after a short burst of activity is one way to test this.

You'll need a bench, or sturdy low chair, 12 to 14 inches from seat to floor. Also get a watch with a second hand.

Begin by standing in a relaxed position, and take a few deep breaths. Now measure your pulse. (You can feel it on the underside of your wrist, about two inches up from the base of your thumb.)

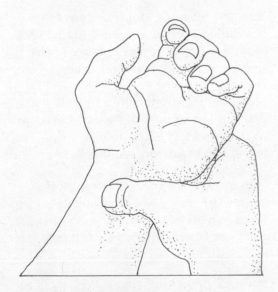

Count the beats for 30 seconds, and double the number. This gives you your starting pulse.

Holding the watch in your hand, step up onto the chair as if you were climbing stairs, one foot and then the other. Then step down one foot at a time. Sound easy? Okay, now try to complete two of these cycles every five seconds.

A cycle is:

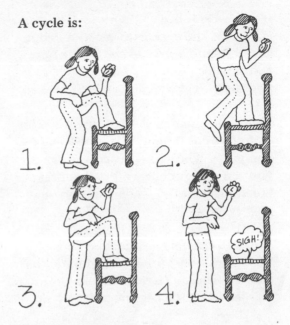

That's 24 cycles a minute!

Count out loud while checking the watch: "One" (up with one foot), "Two" (up with the other foot), "Three" (down with one foot), "Four" (down with the other foot), and so on. It doesn't matter which foot you start or end on.

Keep up this pace for one minute, then sit down and rest for one minute.

Take your pulse again after the one-minute rest. Count the beats for 30 seconds and again double the number. This gives your heart recovery rate. If it's the same or less than the starting rate, your heart is in excellent shape. If it's one or two beats faster, that's still good. Three or four beats faster is fair. Five or six is poor. Seven or more, needs work. Record your before and after rates on the scoresheet.

The 9-Minute Marathon

(Tests heart and lung endurance.)

If you've ever had to "run a lap" in gym class, you know something about endurance. Running uses up endurance fast, and at some point you must stop because your body just won't go an inch farther.

This nine-minute test lets you cheat a bit. You start out running at a slow-to-medium pace. When you get short of breath, you can stop running and walk until your breathing is easier. Then you start running again.

You'll need a measured course to run. The quarter-mile track around a football field is perfect. They're usually already marked along the edge in parts of a mile.

Track Markings:

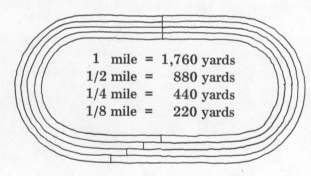

1 mile	=	1,760 yards
1/2 mile	=	880 yards
1/4 mile	=	440 yards
1/8 mile	=	220 yards

You've probably heard these numbers used as short names for running events. The "440," for example, is a quarter-mile run, or once around the track. A track used for races may have several markings for each event. You might see "Lane 1: 220," then farther along "Lane 2: 220," and so on. This is because if all runners start from the same place, the ones toward the outside of the track have to run farther. The staggered finish lines allow for this difference.

For this test, use the track's inside lane. It's the one that will measure exactly a quarter-mile for each complete lap.

If a measured track is not available, you can run along a lightly traveled road. Try to find one with a dirt shoulder. It's easier on your feet than pavement. Telephone poles are good distance markers. They're usually about 50 yards apart.

You can also ask an older friend with a car to drive along the route and measure it with the car's mileage odometer. Tie strips of cloth on posts, or make big chalk marks every quarter-mile. (¼ mile = 2½ tenths on the odometer.) Mark the course for about two miles.

Now put on some tennis or gym shoes, or running shoes if you have them. (See chapter 9 for more about shoes.) Also find a watch with a second hand.

Start running. Remember to walk when you run out of breath, then run again as soon as you feel able. Take it easy. You're not out to break any records yet.

Run for exactly nine minutes. In this amount of time you will probably cover three-fourths of a mile. If you're in very good shape, you might go a full mile, 1¼ miles, or more.

For now though, it's *your* distance that counts. Write it on the scoresheet. More than any other test finding, this one gives you a measure of your overall fitness. As you follow some of the activities in this book, and begin to feel more fit, you can check your progress by taking this test again.

Jack Be Nimble, Jill Be Quick

(A test for agility.)

Agility is the talent for quickly changing direction of movement. It's what allows a small but quick quarterback to dodge a body-bruising tackle, even when the tackler has more speed. Agility is also necessary for a bullfighter to have a long life.

Agility is really a combination of abilities; balance is important; so are speed and strength. To be agile, you've got to be nimble and quick. And the test for agility is a bit like Jack's famous candlestick leap, but with a twist:

Jump from a squat position. Spring into the air with a half-turn, so that you land facing your take-off point. Land with your feet together, and hold your balance for three seconds. Try it several times. One success out of three attempts is passable.

Rolling Stone

(Another test for agility.)

Squat down again, arms outside your knees, hands on the floor. Roll back-ward onto your bottom, then onto your lower back, and up to your shoulders. Keep your knees snug to your chest. Pause, then, keeping your feet close to your bottom, roll forward, returning to the squat position. Then stand up straight. You should be able to complete at least one of these out of three tries.

High Diver

(A test for balance.)

Pretend you're on the high dive. Up on your toes, arms pointed in front of you, eyes closed. Try to hold your balance, without moving your feet, for as long as you can. Count to yourself: "One-thou-sand, two-thousand, three-thousand," etc. Anything over 15 is very good. Less than 5 needs work. Write down your best time.

Hairpin

(A test for flexibility.)

Bend over and try to touch the floor, keeping your knees straight. Can you get hands flat on the floor? Super. Fin-gertips touching? Good. Ankles? Fair. Just below knees? Needs work.

Archer

(Another flexibility test.)

Lie face down on a rug or pad. Clasp your hands behind your neck; extend your elbows. See how far you can raise your chin off the floor. Six inches is fair, 9 inches is good, 12 inches is excellent.

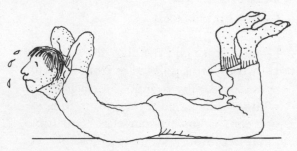

Drag Race

(A speed test.)

Run a measured 50 yards at your top speed. Have a friend time you with a stopwatch, or any watch with a second hand. Record your time.

Leapin' Lizard

(A power test.)

Draw a line in soft dirt, or put a stick down on the grass to mark a starting line. Stand with both feet behind the line. Put your arms out behind you and then swing them forward as you leap. Jump as far as you can. Have a friend measure from the start line to the spot where your heels touch down. Enter the distance on your scoresheet. A distance equal to your height is excellent.

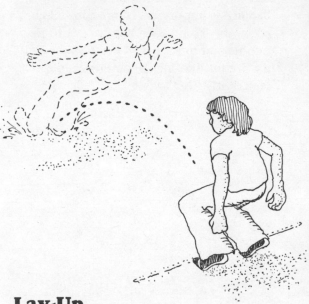

Lay-Up

(A test of jump-and-reach power.)

Find a smooth wall outside. The wall of a handball court is ideal. Stand sideways next to the wall and be sure there's nothing in the way of your reach, above your head, in front, or behind you, for a distance of at least four feet. Place your feet parallel to the wall. Holding a piece of chalk in the hand closest to the wall, and keeping your heels on the ground, reach up as high as possible and make a chalk mark on the wall. This is your baseline.

46

Now squat, swinging your arms back. Bring your arms forward and up as you leap to make a mark as high as you can above the baseline.

Measure the distance between the baseline and the higher mark. Sixteen inches is great; eight inches okay; six inches or less, not so good.

Bridge

(A strength test.)

Lie on the floor, face down, hands flat on the floor, arms bent. Press your body upward. Suspend your weight on your forearms and toes. Hold this position. Twenty seconds is excellent.

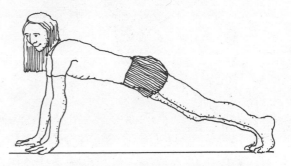

That's it! You now have a pretty complete picture of your body in motion. Make sure your performance scoresheet is all filled out. Then put it someplace safe, or slip it between the pages of this book. You'll want to look at it again, and maybe retest yourself, after you've read other parts of the book.

5

Now Just Relax

(Talking, and Listening, to Your Body)

Remember how you learned to walk?

TO WALK: Assume an upright position. Lock your knees. Raise your left foot. Flex your left leg at the hip. Now swing your leg forward at the knee. (Watch your balance!) Your leg must go out approximately 18 inches. Let the rest of your body start to fall forward, until, (wait until the very last second) your left foot returns to the floor. Keep your body moving forward. Now, lift your right foot . . .

No, if you had been taught to walk the way you're taught almost everything else, you'd probably still be crawling. Instead, you got up, took a few steps, fell a lot, and, within a very short time, you walked.

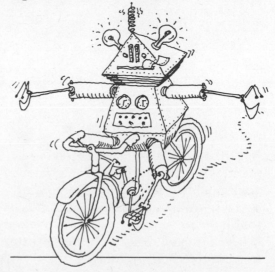

The National Aeronautics and Space Administration has been spending a great deal of time and money to develop a computer, a kind of bionic man, that can do what humans do. But so far NASA technology has failed to develop in this robot the talent for riding a bicycle no-handed.

If this simple human feat is so difficult for a machine to do, maybe being human is more than we take credit for. There are many definitions of being human. In this chapter, think about this one: The human body can be a marvelous, self-correcting, self-teaching machine. It learns many things, all by itself. All you have to do is give it a chance.

Take a minute to consider your body right now. Is it comfortable? Are any parts tense or tight? Close your eyes. Explore your body with your mind.

Say the parts of your body one by one, and ask if they are comfortable and relaxed: "Head — any tension there? Neck — keep it loose. Shoulders — stay relaxed, guys . . . " And so on.

If you've never talked to your body before, it may seem a bit silly at first. Just use your own words, and it's perfectly okay to whisper.

But whatever you say, and however you say it, this simple technique of having your mind talk to your body is very important. Your mind, like all minds, tends to wander all about. Talking to your body helps your mind to *focus*, or pay attention to what your body is doing.

The value of this technique is that when you start talking, you also start listening. You start a two-way conversation in which your body gets a chance to talk back to you. It usually has a lot to say.

Talking, and listening, to your body are a part of just about every relaxation program. And relaxation is the key to letting your body find its own way to learn. Relaxation is the secret ingredient to those amazing breakthroughs, like learning to walk, or riding a bicycle no-handed.

Mind to Body, Over and Out

Here's a simple exercise that will help you start a conversation with your body. Along the way, it also acquaints you with individual muscle groups. This helps you realize where tension is located, and that's the first step to relaxing it.

Lie on your back on a rug or on a folded blanket. (The kind of thin foam sleeping pad used by backpackers is perfect for this and many other exercises in this book.)

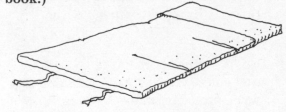

Spread your legs so that your feet are about 12 inches apart. Your arms should lie comfortably alongside your body, palms up, fingers half-closed.

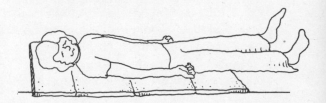

Begin by concentrating on the toes of your left foot. Tense the muscles of your toes as hard as you can, while keeping the rest of your body relaxed.

Think of each muscle in your toes as being the string in an archer's bow. Or imagine that the muscles are the strings of a violin. Tighten them slowly. Talk to the muscles. Tell them to "grow slowly tighter, tighter, now tighter still."

Tense your whole left foot in the same way. Talk to it as it slowly arches and becomes tight and drawn.

Then move on to your left ankle. Move slowly up your left leg, saying the name and telling each part to tighten: "Calf — tighten up. Knee — draw yourself in. Thigh — tighter and tighter. Buttock — tense."

Keeping your left leg tense, check to see that the rest of your body is still relaxed and that your breathing is normal.

Next, tense your right toes, foot, ankle, and so on, as you did with your left leg. Do it slowly, keeping in mind that you are trying to pay attention to each separate muscle group. Work up to your right buttock.

Now, beginning with your fingers, slowly tense your left arm — hand, wrist, forearm, elbow, upper arm, shoulder. Then do your right arm.

Pull in your stomach and tense your trunk, feeling the tightening of the chest muscles. Feel how your breathing becomes harder, but continue to breathe evenly.

Tense your neck muscles and pull your chin in hard.

Screw up your face muscles as tightly as you can.

Now every inch of your body should be drawn as tightly as possible. Imagine that you are a piece of gnarled driftwood. After many years of floating in the ocean, you have washed up high on a deserted beach. The sun has baked you so dry and tight, you feel as though you might crack.

Now, slowly, begin to let go. The tide is coming up the beach, slowly, slowly washing over you. First, it reaches your head. Relax the muscles there. Then the water reaches your shoulders. Relax them. It washes down over your arms and trunk. Then down your legs to your feet.

When you have completely relaxed the last toe, just lie there, breathing quietly, in and out. Your breaths are like gentle waves washing over you, back and forth.

Are you relaxed? Just for fun, take your pulse for 30 seconds after doing this exercise. Double the number, and compare it to your starting pulse before doing the "Go Climb a Chair" exercise (chapter 4). Your slower heartbeat is numerical proof of relaxation.

By the way, if you ever have trouble relaxing enough to get to sleep, this exercise can help. You can do it right in your bed.

For many people in our doing world, relaxing, or *not* doing, is difficult. When you are physically active, your body just naturally gets tired and loose. But when you do *head work* (the kind of work you do in school), your mind gets tired, but your body may actually get even tighter.

The U.S. Navy had this problem of tense bodies with pilots flying long missions. Pilots need intense concentration (head work), and they can't even stretch in the cramped cockpits. Astronauts work under similar conditions.

The Navy's research showed that to relax a muscle you've first got to have a "feel" for it. You have to know the muscle's exact location in your body. Talk-

ing to your body parts, bringing your attention to them, is one way of doing this.

The Navy's method involved two people. One pressed on various muscle groups, one by one, while the other partner responded to the pressure by pushing back. In order to push back, the subject has to develop a "feel" for where the muscle is located.

The Pusher

You can try this with a friend. Ask someone to push gently on the back of your neck, on your shoulders, your calves, and so on. Not only will *you* be able to locate tension, but your friend can find it too. Tense muscles *feel* tense. They're stiff and tight. Your friend may find tension you didn't even know you had. This is also the basis of massage, and that may explain why it is so relaxing.

If you find some tension, what do you *do* about it? Just being aware of tension doesn't make it go away. But once you know where it is, you can do some exercises specially designed to relax the muscles that are stiff. Here are some.

Rubber Neck

You can do this one almost anywhere, while standing or sitting.

Imagine you are a Frankenstein Monster with a steel pin through your neck. Let your head roll forward until your chin hits your chest. Then raise it up and let it fall back, of its own weight, as far as it will go. Repeat, until you feel the muscles relaxing.

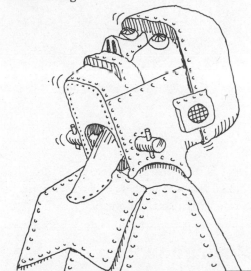

Often, when you're trying something new and difficult, all the effort gets concentrated in the back of your neck. A few "Rubber Necks" are great for loosening that tension.

Shoulder Shrug

That's about it — just shrug your shoulders as high as they'll go. Then let them fall back to where they were.

Now fold your shoulders forward around your chest. And then back, all the way, as if trying to touch your shoulder blades

together. While they're back there, straighten your arms, clasp your hands together, and lift gently against the resistance you feel. Do this whole series of movements several more times, or until your shoulders feel loose.

Back Slacker

From a standing position, bend over and try to touch your fingers to the floor. Bring your head as close as possible to your knees. Come back up, slowly. Raise your arms up and back over your head. Curve your spine back as far as you can. Now return to the starting position and repeat at least once.

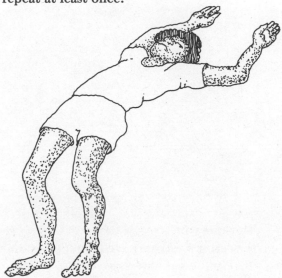

Sometimes, if your whole body is tense, or if specific exercises aren't working, you may need extreme measures. Here is another whole body exercise that fights tension *with* tension.

Magic Carpet

Lie on your back on a bed or on a padded floor. Lift one leg about 12 inches and hold it there. Pretend you are trying to reach something with your toes. Put all your energy and attention into stretching every part of that raised leg while you count slowly to 20. Then drop that leg and immediately lift the other one. Shift your attention to stretching *that* leg for a count of 20, then drop it and quickly raise one arm. Reach out with your arm and fingers as you did with your legs. Count to 20, and then do the same with the remaining arm. Complete the stretching by turning your head from side to side a few times, and then take four deep breaths.

This one works every time. The secret is that after stretching each limb, you completely relax it and *remove it from your thoughts.*

It just lies there, ignored, and therefore fully relaxed. After the deep breaths, you may feel as if your whole body is floating. Then you'll know why it's called the "Magic Carpet."

Now let's suppose you are nowhere near a place where you can lie down. There isn't even time to bend and stretch. For example, you're at bat. The bases are loaded in the bottom of the ninth inning. The pitcher has your number; he's just thrown two high balls that you swung at and missed. You're in an unbearably tense situation. And yet, if you get any tighter, you will surely strike out. What do you do to relax?

There *is* something you can do. But the time to learn it is now, before you get into one of those tight spots.

Blush and Flush

First, check your breathing. Take in full, even breaths and expand your abdomen (stomach). Push the air all the way out before taking the next breath. As you breathe in, imagine you are sending the air directly to the part of your body that feels most tense. For some, that will be the stomach. For others, it's the neck and shoulders.

By just thinking you are breathing to that area, you will open up capillaries (tiny tubes that carry blood). This will actually increase blood circulation, bringing more tension-cleansing oxygen to the tight muscles, and carrying away wastes.

If you wonder how this is possible, think about blushing. For some people the mere suggestion of embarrassment turns them bright red. When they blush, thoughts are opening capillaries and causing more blood to flow.

Your body is constantly telling you things. Once your mind stops to listen, it usually understands and knows what to do. Being relaxed seems to be a matter of just giving your mind permission to listen to, and act on, messages from your body.

6

What's Going On in There?

Have you ever played so hard and so fast that finally you just wore yourself out? What did you do then? If you were really hot and sweaty, your first thought might have been to throw off your jacket. Then you probably collapsed on the ground. There you lay, panting and gasping for breath, your heart pounding so hard you could feel it in your brain.

Now imagine for a minute that you are a scientist examining this simple event from a medical point of view. You observe that there was vigorous exercise, followed by complete exhaustion. The person had four responses to this: (1) took off jacket; (2) flopped down on the ground; (3) lungs gulped in air; (4) heart beat furiously.

Two of these reactions were useful. They helped the body pull itself together. But the other two actions were harmful. They made the body work even harder to recover its energy. Can you decide which actions were good, and which were bad?

This chapter will answer those questions, and a few more. It's about what goes on in your body when you exercise.

Master Muscle

Almost all of your muscles get a workout when you exercise. But there's one muscle that works harder than any other — your heart. Your heart might be called the Master Muscle, because all the other muscles depend on it to bring them blood.

Your heart does one thing, and does it very well: it pumps blood. Blood, on the other hand, does lots of things. Two of its most important jobs are: (1) to carry fresh oxygen to the muscles and organs of the body; and (2) to carry away carbon dioxide, heat, and other waste products, and get rid of them.

The lungs are the garbage dump, as well as the grocery store, for the blood. Here the blood gets as close as it can to the outside air. Here in the lungs the blood dumps its load of wastes, which are breathed out. Then it picks up fresh oxygen from the air you breathe in.

Moving muscles need oxygen in a steady supply. Your body can store food energy. But food is only the fuel. Oxygen is the flame that ignites the stored energy and allows it to be burned.

Oxygen can't be stored. A constant supply must be brought, fresh from the lungs, by way of the bloodstream.

Heart Throbs

Stop reading for a moment and take your pulse.

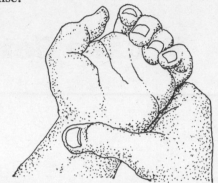

Count the beats for 30 seconds and double the number. This gives your heartbeats per minute *at rest*. Now do a high-stepping run in place for one minute.

Take your pulse again at the end of the minute. This is your *exercise* heart rate. By how much does it exceed your heart rate at rest?

The harder you exercise, the harder your heart must work to bring fresh supplies of oxygen. But there are limits. Your body knows those limits, yet will sometimes go beyond them. But not for long.

When you fall down, exhausted, your body is saying, "I'm broke!" It has overdrawn on its oxygen "bank account," creating a debt that must now be repaid.

Your body calls it quits, but your heart and lungs continue to bring in fresh supplies. The huffing and puffing you do, and your pounding heart, are the outward signs. Inside, your body is busily paying back its *oxygen debt*.

But quitting altogether, crashing in a heap, is not the best way to help your heart and lungs recover. It's been discovered that muscles in your arms and legs can act like miniature hearts if you keep them in gentle motion after exercising. When your muscles are in motion, they massage the blood vessels, gently urging the blood back toward your heart. (Veins actually have little one-way valves. They open to let the blood flow toward your heart, but snap shut if it tries to go the other way.)

Cooling Out

Here's a technique for helping your body pay back its oxygen debt without making your heart work overtime:

Watch runners at a track meet. After an all-out sprinting effort, they'll jog awhile, then walk, and then rest.

It's a good practice to follow any vigorous exercise with a gradually slowed-down version of the same activity. Follow speed skating with slow skating. After swimming hard laps, swim slowly for a while.

The runner's traditional "victory lap" may have originated as a "cooling out" lap. Not only is it a good way to taper off for your heart's sake — it also helps relieve muscle tightness caused by the extra effort of a race.

Swinging your arms above your head, running in place, even slapping your body with your hands — they're all good ways to keep your blood moving after hard exercise.

And don't abruptly shed your clothing after heating up. Blood flows more easily in a warm body. Cold showers are out for the same reason. Stay in your exercise clothes, keep moving, and cool out slowly.

By now you should have the answers to the question at the beginning of this chapter about which reactions are useful and which are harmful. A pounding heart and rapid breathing are your body's proven way of bouncing back from oxygen debt. But taking off your jacket and falling in a heap are, just as clearly, no-nos.

Aerobic / Anaerobic

Don't let these strange-looking words throw you. They come in pretty handy when talking about the effects of exercise on your body.

The kind of exercise that wears you out — that creates oxygen debt — is called *anerobic* (pronounced "an-air-ROW-bic"). The word means "without oxygen."

Short sprints, high-speed swimming, a fast game of basketball — these are all anaerobic activities. They call for speed, power, and strength. A strong heart and large lung capacity are not much help here. In fact, runners of the 100-yard dash sometimes go the whole distance without taking a single breath. It seems that in the burst of speed needed to win such a short race, breathing just gets in the way.

Aerobic (pronounced "air-ROW-bick") means "with oxygen." Aerobic activities use oxygen without using it up. Jogging is an example. Jogging is just fast enough to give your heart and lungs a good workout. When you stop, there's no oxygen debt. You usually don't huff and puff.

Long-distance running and swimming, jumping rope, fast walking, handball, ski touring — all are examples of aerobic activities. In chapter 4, the "Go Climb a Chair" test is anaerobic; "The 9-Minute Marathon" is aerobic.

Any exercise that lasts more than three minutes is probably aerobic. Your body won't let you overdraw your oxygen supply for more than a few minutes. If you start out running at top speed, you'll either have to quit after a short time, or slow to an aerobic pace.

Aerobic Checklist

Make a list of your activities in an ordinary day. If they take lots of energy but last less than three minutes, list them under anaerobic. If they use a fair amount of energy and last more than three minutes, call them aerobic.

You'll probably find that most of your energy goes into anaerobic activities. That makes you even with most Americans, who don't get enough aerobic exercise.

Even if you play tennis, baseball, or football regularly, you may still be lacking in aerobics. The problem is that these are stop-and-go sports. Only the occasional home run, or 85-yard punt return, lasts more than a few minutes. Most of the rest of the time is spent waiting to play. Tennis can be more active, but only if you keep a long volley going.

Anaerobic	Aerobic
1. Brushing teeth.	1. Playing tag.
2. Running to catch bus.	2. Soccer after school.
3. Climbing stairs with books.	3.
4. Raising hand in class.	4.
5.	5.

The Training Effect

To understand the importance of aerobic exercise, you have to take another look at what's going on inside your body.

When you run long distances, or otherwise keep up an exercise for more than three minutes, your body begins to make some changes in the way it operates.

Your breathing becomes slower and deeper as your lungs expand to take on greater amounts of oxygen. Your heart beats faster and also begins to push along more blood with each stroke. This larger blood flow expands the blood vessels. In the area around each muscle, new networks of blood vessels open up. The working tissues are flooded with oxygen, and wastes are carried away more easily.

These amazing adaptations go on as long as you keep moving. But they don't stop there.

Your body remembers what it did to keep up the pace. And the next time, it will be a little wiser. Each time you ask your body to do aerobic exercise, it gains experience in how to handle it. This learning process that your body goes through is called the *training effect*.

Any program designed to improve your overall fitness ought to include some aerobics. Farther along in this book there are some suggestions: running, swimming, and more.

7

A Breath of Life

Have you ever been told: "Stand up straight — don't stoop. You're going to get a humped back!" Parents usually start this chant. And then when you get into gym classes, the p. e. teachers do this variation: "Stand up straight — stomach in, chest out!"

Finally you get the message (sort of). You learn to stand up straight — when adults are watching. The rest of the time you probably relax into your comfortable slouch. Now it appears that your body is wiser than anyone knew.

Research has uncovered the fact that different body types have different natural ways of standing. For instance, most ectomorphs find that a stiff, straight-up-and-down posture is quite unnatural.

But that's not all. When standing in the stomach-in, chest-out position, you force your body to breathe *backwards*. Because your stomach muscles are drawn in, you have to breathe by expanding your chest. Most experts agree that this is the wrong way to breathe.

In "correct" breathing, the kind taught in yoga and many other age-old disciplines, you breathe from the diaphragm up.

Try it. Pretend that you have a hose extending from your nostrils, through your throat, down to your diaphragm.

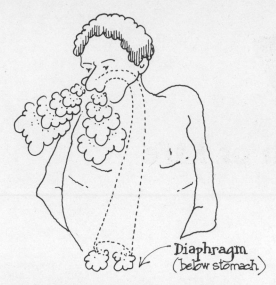

Diaphragm
(below stomach)

Exhale (breathe out) completely, and then inhale (breathe in) through this imaginary tube. Try to let the air drop all the way down to your diaphragm, and fill up from there.

It may help to stand in front of a mirror so that you can see your stomach and chest. Take off your shirt, or put on a T-shirt, so you can really see what's happening.

Make sure, as you inhale, that your stomach expands first, then your chest. If your chest still wants to expand first, practice with a belt around your lower ribs.

Exhale and notch the belt as tight as you comfortably can. Now inhale. The belt will keep your chest in.

This may seem awkward at first, but if you practice this deep breathing (it's the kind you do in your sleep), your lung capacity will gradually increase. You'll find yourself doing better on aerobic exercises. And your heart won't be working so hard either.

Breathing Backwards

Slip the belt down around your belly-button. Exhale, and make the belt comfortably snug.

Now hold the sides of your rib cage and inhale. Use your hands to feel the effort needed to expand your ribs. They will only go so far, and no farther — then the pressure forces you to breathe out.

Breathing with Your Collarbone

Strange as it may sound, many people breathe with their collarbones. The expression "up tight" describes them well.

Try it yourself. You'll need two belts. Put one around your middle and the other around your rib cage. Make the belts moderately tight as you exhale. Now inhale by drawing your collarbone up toward your chin. Difficult, isn't it?

By itself, this kind of breathing takes in the least air, with the most effort. But when combined with deep breathing, to give you a little more "room at the top," it allows for the maximum amount of air to come into the lungs.

Three-Story Breathing

Imagine that your body is like an apartment house: your diaphragm is the basement, your stomach is the first floor, your chest is the second floor, and your collarbone forms the roof over the attic.

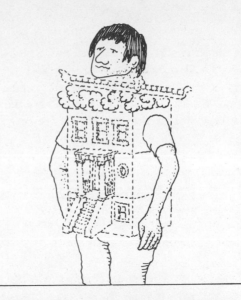

Remove the belts and practice this three-story breathing. Recall the image of the hose leading deep into your stomach. Breathe in, sending the air straight to your "basement." Expand your stomach and let the air slowly fill the "first floor." Then, when your stomach is full, let your chest expand. When you think you can't hold an ounce more air, "raise the roof" and take in a bit more air for the "attic."

Now breathe out slowly, doing everything in reverse. Practice this deep breathing for a few minutes. Some people describe this feeling as "being centered." How does it feel to you?

Record-Breaking Breathing

You'll need a stopwatch, or any watch or clock with a second hand.

Yogis (people who teach yoga) say that the best *breathing ratio* is one to two. In other words, breathing out should take twice as long as breathing in.

Try it. At first, try inhaling for 4 seconds, hold it for a second, and then exhale for

8 seconds. As you become more practiced, extend the inhaling time to 6 seconds — exhaling, 12 seconds; then 8 seconds in, 16 out, and so on. (There may or may not be a world record for this.)

When you've got the basic rhythm, try *holding* your breath. The ratios here are 1:4:2. Start by breathing in for 4 seconds, holding for 16 seconds, and exhaling for 8 seconds. Increase your times slowly, keeping the same ratios.

You can do this yogic deep breathing anywhere: in a classroom, on a bus, before you go to sleep.

Many benefits are claimed for deep breathing. Tests on bicyclelike ergometers prove that people can *train* themselves to take in more oxygen. An athlete in training may be able to inhale twice the amount of air that you or I could.

Lungs themselves have no muscles. They only expand to fill the space made available. Deep breathing actually develops the muscles around the lungs, and it's these muscles that can be taught to expand and contract more.

Other ideas about deep breathing cannot be easily tested. Some Asians consider breathing to be almost a religious experience. They have a word that carries this meaning: In Japan it's *ki*, as in Ai*ki*do. And in China it's *c'hi*, the life-energy released by T'ai Chi Ch'uan. Roughly translated, the word means "breath of life."

To Asians, breathing is our most essential meeting with the outside world. Every time we breathe, we inhale a piece of our surroundings. We take it in, change it, then give it back to the world.

Our own word *spirit* is maybe the closest to that meaning. It comes from an old Latin word: *spiritus*, which meant "breath of a god."

66

Now Let Your Lungs Breathe You

Take a deep breath, and then exhale through your mouth, until you are completely empty. Then, instead of taking a breath, just close your mouth and *wait*. You don't have to think in order to breathe. The incoming breath arises naturally when your body is ready.

Magda Proskauer, a woman who teaches people how to breathe, calls this the "creative pause." She observes that the breath comes as a delightful surprise, and a gentle reminder: "I'll take care of this," says your body to your mind.

Breathe deeply. It's good for your health, and your spirit.

T'ai Chi Ch'uan

(Pronounced: "TIE-GEE-CHWAHN" — all three words are given the same emphasis.)

T'AI CHI is a Chinese martial art involving gentle stretching like yoga. Watching it might make you think of shadow-boxing. In fact, one English translation of T'ai Chi Ch'uan is: "The Ultimate Art of Boxing." Another possible translation is "The Perfect Art of Nothing!" That should give you a feeling for what the translators are up against.

CHANG SAN-FENG, a Chinese monk who lived about a thousand years ago, is said to be the inventor of T'ai Chi. As legend has it, Chang was in the house meditating at noon when a strange sound arose from the courtyard...

Looking down from his window, Chang saw a snake with raised head. It was hissing, challenging a crane in the tree above. As Chang watched, the crane flew boldly down and attacked the snake with its swordlike beak. The snake turned its head aside and slashed at the bird's neck with its tail. The crane used its wing to protect its neck.

Then the snake darted against the bird's legs. The crane raised its left leg and lowered its left wing to block the attack. Stabbing again and again, the bird was unable to make a solid blow. The snake, twisting and bending, was always out of reach.

Soon both animals tired of the evenly matched contest. The crane flew up into the tree, and the snake slithered back into its hole. They rested for the next encounter.

CHANG SAN-FENG observed this duel from his window again and again. From watching this strange battle he realized the value of yielding in the face of strength. The great master observed other animals as well, and the clouds, the water, and the trees bending in the wind. He studied and organized these natural movements into a system of exercise. From the action of the crane came a movement called White Crane Spreads Wings:

FROM the action of the snake came Snake Creeps Down:

HE constructed other forms based on other movements he had seen and put them together in the gentle martial art we know as T'ai Chi Ch'uan.

T'ai Chi Stance

ALL of T'ai Chi is done from a balanced standing position. Feet are moderately apart, knees are slightly bent, arms hang at your sides. Try it.

HOLD your spine straight, yet easily, as if you were suspended from a point at the very top of your head.

TRY to feel your whole body hanging loosely from this point. Your jaw may relax and your tongue should rest lightly against your palate. Feel that you don't need as much energy as you usually use to support your body.

NOW extend your fingers. Don't curl them, but keep them relaxed. Try to feel rays of energy shooting from your fingertips, as if they were hose nozzles with water rushing out of them.

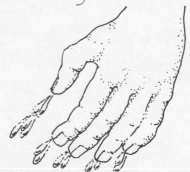

T'AI CHI is a gentle, stretching exercise. When all the movements flow, one after another, it appears to be a dance. T'ai Chi draws on inner strength. As a woman who teaches the art says: "You don't see big muscles, but inside they are strong."

8

Yoga
(A "Perfect" Exercise)

Do you know what a consumer is? It's someone who buys and uses things. The word is sometimes used even for people who buy and use information. That would include you, since you have bought (or borrowed) and are using the information in this book.

As the consumer of this book, you might be questioning the title of this chapter. (Consumers can't be too skeptical these days.) What, you might ask, makes an exercise "perfect"?

Of course, no exercise is perfect unless it's right for you. But the following test can help you decide what *is* right for you. It's sort of a "consumer's guide" to exercise.

In Search of a Perfect Exercise

An exercise tends toward perfect if it passes the following tests:

1. Is it for your whole body?
2. Does it involve slow stretching rather than violent, strenuous activity? (If your exercise tires you, you'll be reluctant to do it regularly.)

3. Do you feel better right after doing it? How about the next day?

4. Is it non-competitive? Are you the only judge of when you've had enough?

5. Is it for everyone? If it passes the other tests, it will also be comfortable for anyone, male or female, old or young, to do.

6. Is the exercise possible for you to do (at least with some practice)?

7. Can you do it by yourself, without complicated preparation or equipment? Any time? Any place?

8. Is it fun?

Do you ever watch football on TV? Sometime tune in early and watch how the pros do their warm-up exercises these days. The old "herky-jerky" calisthenics have gone the way of leather helmets.

The San Francisco 49ers, The Los Angeles Rams, and other pro clubs have completely done away with traditional calisthenics. Now they're doing slow, even, stretching exercises.

What they're doing is based on *yoga*, though they may not call it that. Through trial and injury, football players have rediscovered one of the world's oldest movement disciplines. But where the true *yogis* are using these stretching and breathing exercises to reach a higher kind of spirituality, the 49ers have a more earthbound ambition.

The pros have adopted *yogic* exercise simply because it works. The slow, stretching exercises prepare players in advance for the strenuous activity of the game. They actually help prevent injuries. For us non-professionals, yoga, combined with an endurance program, like running, can be the perfect exercise.

There are many different kinds of yoga. Mantra Yoga is study through chanting and sounds. Karma Yoga is the discipline of work and service. Kundalini Yoga is a whole system of knowledge about the energy in the human spine.

Physical yoga, the kind football players are doing, is called Hatha Yoga — yoga for health. When people talk generally about yoga, they usually mean Hatha Yoga.

Hatha Yoga is not too difficult, and it requires very little equipment, but it does have a few rules. Most important is breathing. Deep breathing is half of the whole purpose of yoga, but it's the hardest part to get right. To help you get it right from the start, look for these little symbols as you read the directions for each exercise:

◯ means "Breathe out as you do this."

⦷ means "Breathe in as you do this."

A second rule for good yoga practice is to be relaxed. A simple relaxing exercise, like "The Magic Carpet" (chapter 5), puts your mind and your body in a good place for yoga.

If you are doing yoga alone, pick a time and place where your concentration will not be disturbed. At one time yoga was always done as a solitary activity. (Maybe because it was first used by monks.) Now many people like to do yoga in groups. However you and your group do yoga, make sure everybody in the room is doing it.

No spectators.

Salute to the Sun

In India, dedicated students of Hatha Yoga practice this exercise at dawn, facing east, just as the sun rises. Coming from sleep, they use this time to "get back into" their bodies, stretching the spine and the muscles, and deepening their breathing.

The Salute feels good any time of day. There are 12 movements to the complete exercise, but don't expect to go right through them the first time. Do one movement, check the directions, and then add another part. A half-hour is not too long to spend learning a new yoga exercise.

1. Stand relaxed, feet together. Arms should be at your sides or folded in front of your chest in the prayer position. ◯ (Breathe out slowly.)

2. ⦷ (Breathe in slowly as you . . .) Raise your arms over your head. Stretch back as far as you comfortably can.

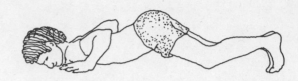

3. ◯ Bend forward and place your hands on the floor. If you can't put your hands flat on the floor, try to touch with just your fingertips. Bring your head as close as possible to your knees as you stretch downward.

6. ◯ Lower your body to the floor (as if you were coming down from a push-up), keeping your bottom up in the air so you are touching the floor at only eight points: forehead, two hands, chest, two knees, and toes.

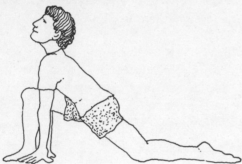

4. ◑ Shift your weight to your hands by flexing your knees. Stretch your left leg backward and touch the toes to the floor. While your right knee is bent, keep your right foot flat on the floor between your hands. ◯

7. ◑ Supporting yourself on your hands, knees, and toes, bend backward from your waist. This pose, when done by itself, is called the Cobra. Hold it, stretching gently back a little more. Breathe in and out a few times. ◯ ◑ ◯ ◑

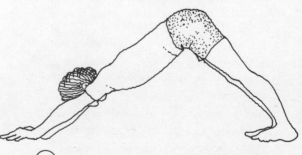

5. ◑ Stretch your right leg back, keeping your body in a straight line from head to heels.

8. ◯ Lift your bottom high up in the air, but keep your hands and feet flat on the floor. If your heels rise up, gently

stretch them downward, one at a time. This limbers up the Achilles tendons. Hold this position while breathing in and out a few times. ⊕ ◯ ⊕ ◯
This is the Dog pose.

9. ⊕ Bring your right leg forward and tuck your knee under your chin. ◯

10. ⊕ Bring your left leg forward. Both feet should now be between your hands again. Your chin should be pressed against your knees. ◯

11. ⊕ Stand slowly and raise your arms over your head once again.

12. ◯ Return to your starting position. Relax and breathe deeply several times.
⊕ ◯ ⊕ ◯ ⊕ ◯

The Shoulder Stand and the Plow

Yoga exercises are called *asanas*. This is a double asana which uses almost all of your major muscle groups. And because it puts your feet and trunk above your head, it's also good for your circulation.

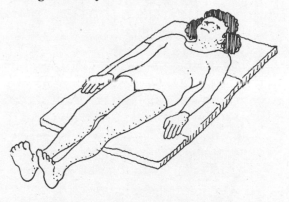

1. Lie on your back on a pad, rug, or folded blanket. Your hands should be lying at your sides, palms down. Breathe in and out a few times to get a rhythm going. ◯ ⊕ ◯ ⊕

2. ◯ Raise your legs slowly. Keep your thighs relaxed and let your stomach muscles do most of the work.

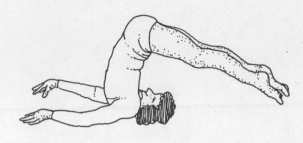

7. ⦶ Bring it up.

8. ◯ Lower both legs toward the floor. Flex your knees, if necessary, so that both big toes can touch the floor. Extend your arms again for support. Hold and breathe.

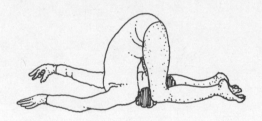

⦶◯⦶◯ This is the Plow.

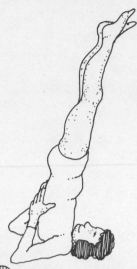

3. ⦶ Without stopping, let the rest of your body follow your legs up in the air until your spine and legs make a straight line. Support yourself by holding your back with your hands. Your elbows and your shoulders form the three points of a stable tripod. This is the Shoulder Stand.

◯⦶◯⦶

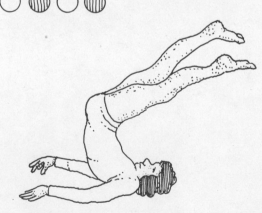

9. ⦶ Now bend your knees to bring them down next to your ears. Hold.

◯⦶◯⦶

4. ◯ Slowly lower one leg behind your head to the floor, or as near the floor as you can get.

5. ⦶ Bring that leg back up.

6. ◯ Lower the other leg.

10. ◯ Slowly straighten your legs and begin to uncurl. Pretend you are a carpet slowly unrolling itself on the floor.

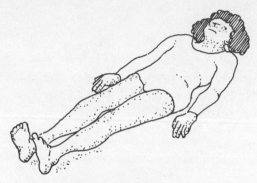

your toes under your bottom and grasp your heels with your hands. ◯

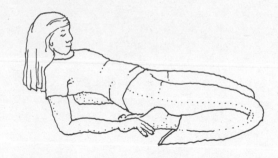

11. (Optional.) When your legs are almost down, stop and hold them a few inches above the floor. ⬙ ◯ ⬙ ◯

12. ⬙ Let your legs down and relax completely. Take a well-deserved rest. Breathe in and out deeply. ◯ ⬙ ◯ ⬙ , etc.

2. ⬙ Lean back and to one side, catching your backward movement with one elbow. Go on back so you're leaning on both elbows. ◯ ⬙

The Fish

Asanas are often meant to complement each other. The Fish is a good one to follow the Shoulder Stand and Plow. It bends the spine in the opposite direction. It's also good for toning up thighs and buttocks.

3. ◯ Lean your head back as far as you can. Arch your chest and back.

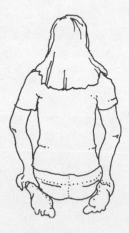

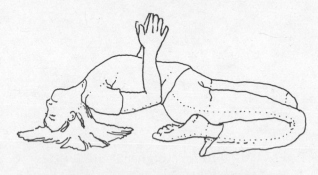

1. Sit on your heels. Keeping your knees together, move your feet apart so that you're sitting *between* your heels. Tuck

4. ⬙ Fold your hands over your chest, and support your body only on your folded legs and the top of your head. Hold for about ten breaths. ◯ ⬙ ◯ ⬙ , etc.

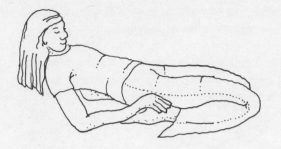

5. ◯ Hold your heels again and rise to your elbows.

6. ▥ Come back up to a sitting position lifting one elbow at a time.

7. ◯ Without stopping, bend forward and touch your head to your knees, or as close as you can get. Hold. ▥ ◯ ▥ ◯ ▥ ◯

8. ▥ Return to your starting position.

The Bow

The Bow is not easy to do. In fact, it's included in this brief sampling of asanas partly because it *is* difficult. Try the Bow and you will realize that even if yoga appears to be gentle and slow it's not "sissy stuff."

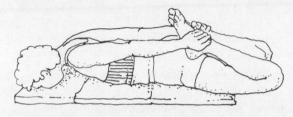

1. Padding is very necessary for this one, especially for ectomorphs. Lie on your stomach and bend your legs so that you can grip your ankles. The positioning of the hands is shown in the drawing. ◯ ▥

2. ◯ Push your feet back and up. This will lift your head and your hips so that you are balanced on your stomach.

3. ▥ Rock gently back and forth. Easy does it the first time. A little of this goes

a long way. Make sure you are breathing normally. Keep your arms straight but relaxed. ◯ ◍ ◯ ◍

4. ◯ Stop rocking, hold briefly, then return to lying on the floor. Rest and breathe deeply. ◍ ◯ ◍ , etc.

Not only does yoga stretch and release tension in muscles and tendons, but it also changes circulation (as when you're upside down). Yoga works in more hidden ways, too, on nerves and glands of the body. The electrical and chemical centers of the body are stimulated, causing you to feel alive, well, and different, in almost magical ways.

Yoga is very thorough and complete. It makes you feel good. You might even find it's a perfect exercise.

In the five thousand years that yoga has been around, more than one hundred asanas and variations have been developed. The four given here are only a taste of what the teaching has to offer. And yet, if you only do these four, but do them every day, you'll begin to feel changes almost immediately. Yoga is powerful medicine.

Yoga on the Gridiron

JERRY COLLETTO is coach of the Junior Varsity football team at Novato High School in California. This is how he explains his involvement in both football and yoga:

"**A**LL my life I have loved sports. My interest in tennis started when I was seven years old. The next year I played Little League baseball.

"**W**HEN I was a freshman in high school I weighed 98 pounds, but I went out for football anyway. The coach tried to cut me, but I went to him in tears and convinced him of my determination to be on the team. I got a uniform. When we were dressing for road games and I heard the coach call my name, I knew it was because some other player had forgotten a piece of equipment and the coach wanted to give him mine.

"**I** was manager for varsity basketball during my freshman year in high school so that I could be involved with the sport. In my junior year I played in the preliminary games in football and came back as a cheerleader for the varsity games.

"**W**HAT does all this past history have to do with yoga? Mostly it goes to show that I was raised in the same 'grit your teeth and try

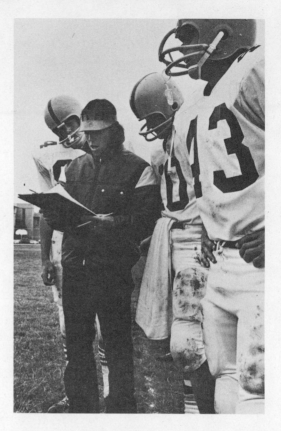

extra hard' tradition as most other American athletes. When I started studying yoga several years ago a new dimension was added to my sports life.

"**O**NE of the things I find most beautiful about sports is the experience of reaching down into myself for a hidden reserve that supports an extra effort. Maybe I find I'm able to run a little faster, or twist or stretch in a new direction, or move my body into position with more agility. Yoga conditioning exercises make greater physical and mental effort possible. In addition, the mind control that hatha yoga practice lends an athlete allows him or her to fully experience the testing of limits that sports and life provide. Many people who practice yoga achieve a kind of stillness of mind that allows them to experience the complete use of their bodies and minds in play.

"ONE interesting example of this sort of experience occurred this past winter when my family went skiing. It was my first trip of the season. On the first few runs I became so absorbed with the techniques of bending my knees just right, planting the pole just right, leaning forward, and unweighting my skis that I actually forgot to enjoy skiing. I noticed that I wasn't getting any better with the attention to details and technique. So I just let the details go and got into a flowing, smooth place with my skiing the way I do with yoga. Soon I found myself skiing much better. I was almost as one with the snow and the skis. And my movements became rhythmical and seemed slow and very positive."

JERRY COLLETTO uses the asanas in chapter 8 with his team, as well as many others. He also prescribes the following balance exercises. They're especially good for linemen to do, since they do most of their moving in very limited space. Tennis and volleyball players can also benefit from exercises like these.

Flying Stork

PULL your knee and ankle up as high as you can while pushing out with your foot. Lean forward slightly and raise your other arm up as high as possible. Tilt your head back. Now repeat using the opposite side of your body.

One Foot Squat

THIS one teaches composure and concentration. It's not easy. Squat on your toes. Put one hand down for balance and use the other to pull your left foot up so it's resting on your right thigh. Now carefully bring your hands up in front of your chest. It helps to concentrate on your breathing and look off to the horizon. Relax.

9
Run with the Wind

If you think running is just something to do when you're scared, Mike Spino could change your mind. Mike *teaches* people how to run.

Mike loves to run, but hates to jog. He thinks jogging is monotonous. "Think about play," he says. "Play is fun, because it's always changing. But what does *jogging* bring to mind: jarring, repetition, boredom?"

"Running is one of the best aerobic exercises," Mike says, "but don't take it too seriously!" He thinks people are not playful enough about running. They go out every day, run the same distance, at the same pace. The secret of *playful* running is to vary the pace, and the place.

Did You Ever See a Horse Jog?

Mike thinks that we can learn a lot about running by watching animals. "Horses run and breathe in a free-flowing, unplanned way. That's about as far as you can get from the stiff, locked-elbows approach of most Sunday-joggers."

Vary Your Pace

1. Start with a *shuffle*. It's a little faster than walking. Your feet slide forward, your heels barely leave the ground. Take short steps, letting your heels touch first, before your toes. Let your arms swing loosely at your sides.

3. Now try a *good swing tempo*. Lift your knees and step out, landing on the outsides of your feet, then rolling in toward the centers. Your arms are at your sides, swinging easily.

2. After a few minutes, switch to a *canter*. Your knees come up higher. Your arms stand out, moving in circles ahead of you.

4. Follow with a *good speed tempo*. Your hands are carried just below your chest. They move up and down together. Your feet should meet the ground just behind your toes.

Don't worry about duplicating these styles exactly. Every horse, and every person, runs a little bit differently. Find the style that feels right for you. Keep experimenting, and keep it fun.

Athletes from all different sports have turned to running as the best exercise for increasing endurance. It could be what you need, too, to help build up your heart and lungs. But keep this in mind: the key to running (and to many other sports) is in not trying too hard.

5. The *sprint form*, or *power run*, pushes the body hard. It supplies anaerobic, or oxygen debt, training, so you'll want to do this for only short distances. Knees come up as high as your waist. Arms swing all the way forward and back.

Look at Lee Evans, a world-class runner. There's strength in those arms and legs, for sure. But also look at his wrists, hands, and face. They're surprisingly relaxed, almost casual.

Here are some of Mike Spino's suggestions for running relaxed:

Let your tongue "flap" in your mouth as you run. Keep your face and jaws loose. It also helps to touch your thumb to your index finger as you run. Somehow, doing this forces your upper arms to stay loose and relaxed.

What to Run On

(best to worst)

1. Cut grass.
2. Dirt along the side of a road.
3. Pavement. (If you must run on pavement, wear thick, rubber-soled shoes.)

What to Run In

Get a pair of running shoes if you can. Good nylon shoes cost from 6 to 12 dollars. Tennis shoes, or sneakers, are the next best. Make sure there is plenty of room in the toes (about ½ to ¾ inch). Wear thick socks to soak up the sweat and to help prevent blisters.

If you run in the rain, you're better off with no socks. They get soggy and can cause real pain. Your shoes will tend to shed the water and to dry out quickly when the rain stops.

Go Slow

If you find that you are indeed a "born runner" (it is said that some people *must* run, as others *must* write), then by all means, *run*. But take it easy. The rule is: warm up slowly, run relaxed, and cool out slowly. If you do a lot of running, be sure to include stretching exercises as part of your warm-up routine.

Running strengthens, but also tightens, the calf and hamstring muscles. As they tighten, they put extra strain on the Achilles tendon. Here's an exercise to help keep those tendons loose and supple.

Leaning Tower

Stand about two feet from a wall. Straighten your arms, lean forward, and put your palms against the wall. Now, without moving your feet or lifting your heels, let your body lean forward. If it hurts, and you must lift your heels, stop and move your feet closer to the wall.

Make this exercise a part of your warm-up for running.

Run for Your Life

Here's a program to get you running — a little faster and a little farther each week. (Also see chapter 4 for tips on running measured courses.)

WEEK	DISTANCE (in miles)	WALK OR RUN	TIME GOAL (in minutes)	FREQUENCY (per week)
1	1.0	Walk	12:45	5
2	1.0	Walk/Run	11:00	5
3	1.0	Walk/Run	10:30	5
4	1.0	Run	9:30	5
5	1.0	Run	9:15	5
6	1.0	Run	8:45	3
	and 1.5	Run	15:00	2
7	1.0	Run	8:30	3
	and 1.5	Run	14:00	2
8	1.0	Run	7:55	3
	and 1.5	Run	13:00	2
9	1.0	Run	7:45	2
	and 1.5	Run	12:30	2
	and 2.0	Run	18:00	1
10	1.5	Run	11:55	2
	and 2.0	Run	17:00	2

A few more tips about running: If you feel pain, stop. Pain is your body's signal that you're pushing it too hard.

On the other hand, it's okay to feel tired and to keep on running. Very often the tiredness will go away as your body changes to meet the steady demand for energy. Runners call this the *second wind*.

There's another kind of wind that can help you when you're tired. It's the wind that you can imagine blowing at your back, urging you on. Mike has several of these "imaginary helpers." He calls on them to keep him going, when he'd really rather stop: Pretend that a giant hand is pushing you along, or that you're running downhill. Imagine that the ground is moving under you. All you have to do is put your feet down, and it will carry you along.

These are all ways to get in touch with extra energy you didn't know you had.

Soccer: Everybody Plays

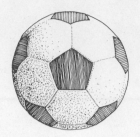

DID YOU ever try out for a team sport? Did you notice that they usually pick the people who are already good? Then, those who make it through the try-outs are further divided into first-, second-, and third-string teams. Now guess who gets to be on the first string and do most of the playing? You've got it. The players who are already the best. And so they get better. The rest of us go off and read books.

AYSO is a group that's trying to turn this all around. AYSO stands for American Youth Soccer Organization, whose motto is "Everybody plays." There are over four thousand teams in California, and hundreds more in Hawaii, Oregon, Arizona, Utah, Kansas, Michigan, and Connecticut.

AYSO soccer teams are like Little League or Pop Warner football, except for one big difference: every kid on every team gets to play at least half of every game. The teams have attracted lots of kids, girls and boys, who didn't dare try out for Little League because they felt too shy or clumsy.

GIVEN half a chance, most kids find they're not as uncoordinated as they thought. Soccer doesn't put you in a spot where you either get a hit or you strike out. It's not even possible to fumble the ball. When the pressure to be a star is removed, everybody seems to play better.

SUSIE BAIRD plays on a Northern California team. A year ago she didn't even play games at recess. Now she's on a championship soccer team and she's much more interested in <u>everything</u>.

BEST player on the Eagles last season was 10-year-old Maria Gutierrez. She was 4'5", weighed 67 pounds, and scored 52 goals. Maria is the kind of player who gets "redistributed" in AYSO soccer. At the end of each season the coaches rate their most experienced players, and the two or three top players from each team are shifted to other teams in the area.

FOR every three kids on an AYSO team, there's at least one volunteer adult. And instead of one all-powerful head coach, there are multiple adult helpers for kids to relate to. For the most part, these adults don't get wrapped up in win-loss records and statistics. They are there to make sure everybody gets a chance to kick a soccer ball and have a good time.

IF you'd like to get your own AYSO region started, you can write to:

American Youth Soccer Organization
4015 Pacific Coast Highway
Torrance, California 90505

10

Weight and See

What do you imagine when you see the words *weight training?* Do you picture a muscle-bound giant? It used to be that "lifting weights" meant the same as "body building." But "real athletes" didn't go in for that show-business, Mr. America stuff. Some coaches even thought weight lifting was harmful to athletes. They felt that it added extra weight and bulk without actually improving performance.

But there's a difference between weight *training* and weight *lifting.*

Weight lifting, or "pumping iron" as it's sometimes called, is a sport in itself. Scoring is based on lifting the greatest amount of weight. Some of these heavy-weight-class lifters are roly-poly giants weighing over 300 pounds. It's probably from observing these heavyweights that coaches got the idea that weight lifting adds unwanted bulk as well as strength.

Bulk isn't always a problem. Strength *does* increase with muscle size, to a

point. But weight training *can* build strength without producing bulging muscles.

Training with weights has become a standard part of getting in shape for almost every sport. Runners do it. Swimmers do it. Even volleyball players are training with weights to improve their strength and jumping power.

Gus Mee, who played on the U.S. volleyball team in the 1973 World Games in Moscow, is only six feet one inch tall. With weight training he was able to increase his jump about 8 inches, so that he could leap and touch a mark 11 feet high!

Weight training is something you might want to take or leave. If you're not bound for the Olympics, you may never really need to touch a barbell. For casual sports, flexibility exercises (like yoga) and aerobics (like running) will probably give you all the conditioning you'll need.

But besides building strength in specific muscles, lifting weights can be fun.

A Weighty Problem

Beautiful weight-training equipment — dumbbells, barbells, benches, and the like — can be purchased ready-made. The only problem with this factory-made gear is that it's too expensive. A way around this is presented in chapter 12, where there are plans for building your own weight-training equipment.

Some Rules

Weight training *can* be painful. It's not like running, where your body tends to get tired before it gets hurt. Here are some cautions for injury-free weight training:

Warm up: Do stretching exercises, like yoga, for five or ten minutes before beginning to lift weights. The first weight exercise should be a continuation of the warm-up. Use a light enough weight so that you can easily do about 25 repetitions.

Start light: Newcomers to weight training should use only very light weights.

(About 5 percent of your body weight for dumbbells. About 10 percent for barbells.) Work first at developing good form. Don't repeat exercises to the point of fatigue. Resist the temptation to show off. If your muscles ache for one or two days after the workout, so that you are reluctant to repeat the training, you're doing too much.

Alternate: While resting from one exercise, do another that uses different muscles. For example, after a set of leg exercises, do an arm exercise as a "breather."

Don't be a drudge: Weight training should not be an everyday routine. For best strength training, do a series of four or five exercises three days a week. You *do* need to stick to it, though. In weight training, "staying power" is more important than "lifting power."

Weight Training Without Weights

(Bent-leg situps.)

In this exercise it's your own upper body that provides the weight. And it's your abdominal muscles (the ones around your stomach) that do the lifting.

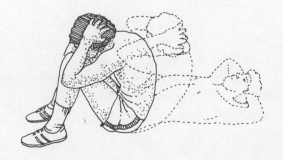

Lie on your back, on a rug or pad. Bend your knees and cradle your head in your hands. Keeping your feet on the floor, *roll* up (don't jerk) until your forehead is between your knees. Do 5 to start. Work up to 15 or 20. While you strengthen your abdominal muscles, you're also helping prevent lower back pains. The abdominal muscles, being in your middle, are also involved in most other kinds of movement. So a strong midsection is a help toward overall fitness.

The Half-Squat

This is a little like getting up from a chair with your kid brother on your shoulders. It's one of the best all-around weight exercises, especially good for the upper legs.

You'll need a barbell loaded to equal about one-third of your body weight.

Lift the barbell over your head and onto your shoulders, or have a *spotter* (a friend) help hold the weight while you get under it.

With your feet about shoulder-width apart, your back straight, and your head up, bend your legs until your thighs are parallel to the floor. Then return to the starting position and repeat. To make

sure you don't go too far down, place a chair so that you just sit on the edge in the lowest part of the squat.

If the weight seems too heavy for you, if you feel off-balance, or have to jerk, or otherwise have to break your form — stop. Use a lighter weight.

Do 12 repetitions to start. Work toward squatting with half of your body weight, and doing two sets of 12 repetitions.

Forearm Curl

Strong forearms help take the strain away from wrist and elbow joints. This is a good exercise for tennis players, or anyone who throws and catches a ball.

You need a five-pound dumbbell.

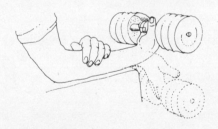

Rest your arm flat on a table so that your wrist extends over the edge. Your palm should be up. Grasp the dumbbell and slowly lift it in your hand as high as possible, without raising your arm. You may have to hold your forearm down with your other hand. Now lower your hand slowly, all the way. Repeat. Work up to 25 repetitions.

Do the same exercise with your palm down. Work up to 25 times. When this is easy for you, increase the weight. But don't go beyond 10 percent of your body weight.

The Bench Press

This is the complete weight-training exercise for the upper body, a good alternate with the Half-Squat.

You'll need a barbell loaded to one-third of your body weight, and a sturdy, chair-height bench. A board laid across two chairs and padded with a folded blanket can serve as a bench. Make sure it's sturdy.

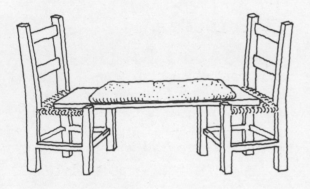

Have your spotter friend, or friends, hand you the barbell after you are lying down on the bench.

Keep your back flat, your hands slightly wider than your shoulders. Lower the bar until it touches your chest, and then press it up until your arms are straight. Go slowly. The muscles benefit from both lowering and pressing (or lifting) the weight.

Breathing is as important here as in any exercise. Inhale as you lower the weight. Exhale as you press upward (maximum exertion). This breathing pattern works well for other weight training exercises too.

Depth Jump

This is an exercise that develops strength and power in the leg muscles. It's especially good conditioning for jumping sports, like basketball, volleyball, and the high jump.

The exercise is tiring for the legs, so it should be saved for the end of any training session.

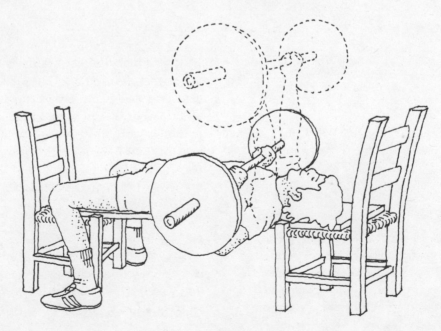

Stand on a table about 30 inches high, and then jump onto a soft gym mat. Outdoors, jump into sand or soft earth. As soon as you land, jump up as high as you can. The faster you can jump up after jumping down, the more good this exercise will do. Work up to 15 or 20 jumps.

Caution: Jumping onto a hard surface can cause a knee injury.

Steady weight training is work. And it's specialized work. But it's a good feeling, sometimes, to put a lot of effort into improving one thing. If you want to be stronger, weight training will do it.

Chairman Mao's Fitness Program

AT the appointed hour, the sound of a bugle crackles from the public loudspeakers. Early in the morning and twice during the workday, students and workers all over China pause to do their exercises. The bugle ends, and as the echo dies away a voice proclaims, in the words of Chairman Mao Tse-tung:

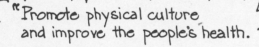

"Promote physical culture and improve the people's health.

"Heighten our vigilance, defend the motherland."

THIS is followed by sprightly marching music. It sounds like something from the musical *South Pacific* played through an old car radio. The exercises are performed in time to the music.

TO you or me this may be too much like summer camp, or maybe the Army. But Americans who have toured China come back very impressed by the excellent health and good humor of the Chinese people.

THESE exercises grew out of a program of body workouts that Chairman Mao devised first for his own use. Mao believed his country could not be whole until every individual felt the strength and courage its leaders felt. Strength of mind, he thought, could only exist in strong bodies.

YET for all the emphasis on strength and militarylike discipline, Chairman Mao's exercises are quite calm and gentle. They can be done by males and females, old and young. In fact they meet all the tests for a perfect exercise. Done to music, they're even fun. (Any basic 4/4 music will do. The tempo is about 100 beats per minute. The Beatles' song *Sergeant Pepper's Lonely Hearts Club Band* is good for starters.)

THE program begins with 32 steps in place. Do them briskly, in time with the music. Here are directions for doing two of the eight exercises in the complete series:

Exercise 1: STAND arms beside you, palms in. Look straight ahead. Feet are turned out, heels together. At step 1 the left leg steps out. At 2, arms reach straight up. At 3, bring arms down, then reach out. Return to starting position and repeat with the right leg.

Exercise 2: START as in exercise 1. At step 1 the body turns 90° to the left, and the left leg makes a big step out. At 2, right arm punches straight out. At 3, left arm punches out. Return to starting position and repeat using right leg.

THE benefit from these exercises is close to that gained by doing yoga. This is a flexibility and muscle toning program. For cardiovascular (heart and lung) training, you'll need to add an aerobic exercise like running.

BEFORE leaving China we should pay respects to the highly developed sportsmanship there. In China when teams come together to compete, they stand facing each other and say:

"Friendship first, competition second."

Then each team repeats, in turn:

"We learn from you."

They shake hands and begin playing. If during the game there is a foul or any other breaking of the rules, the players involved apologize and shake hands again. Can you picture that happening in an American hockey game?

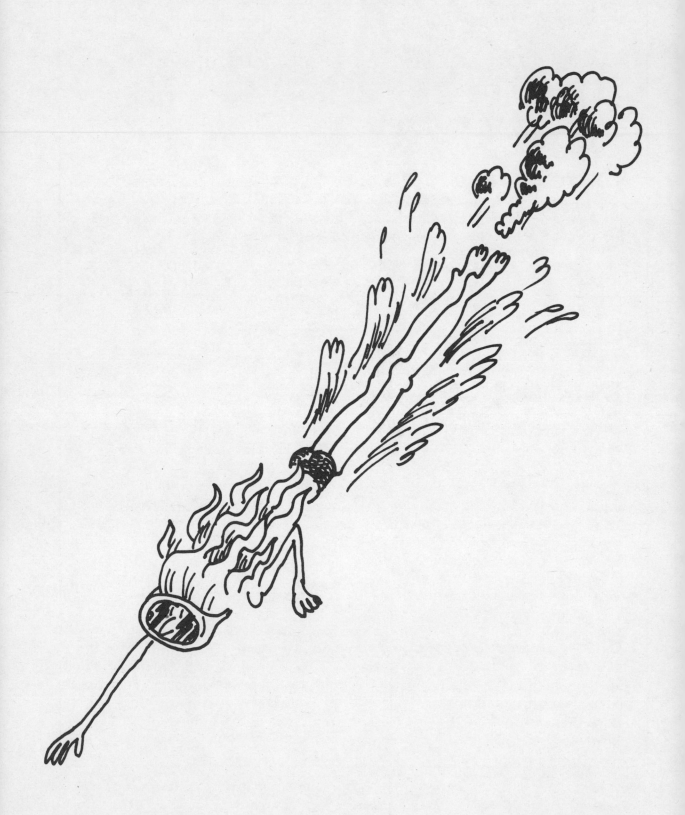

11

New Swimming

You can't learn to swim by reading this chapter. But you *can* find out about a few techniques that may help you swim better.

Rosie Menninger is a young woman who learned to swim in the old ways. At first, new ideas about swimming were scary to her. "When you've already learned how to swim," she says, "it's pretty threatening to find out that you might have done it all wrong."

Rosie compares it to an old car:

The square shape has to batter its way through the air. So does a swimmer who swims too low in the water. New swimmers are like new cars. They're

streamlined. Swimming higher lets you skim *over* the water instead of wasting effort plowing through it.

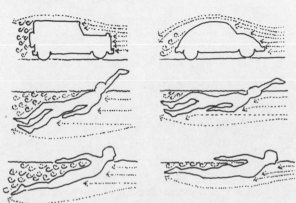

99

It's kind of like the difference between a whale and a flying fish.

When *you* swim, are you a flying fish or a whale? One way to find out is to get a pair of swimming goggles:

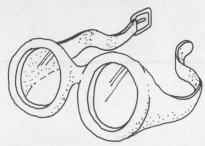

Goggles let you see what you're doing in the water. Comparing your clear view of yourself swimming with the pictures of correct strokes from a book can help you to change. Rosie credits her goggles as one of her two most helpful teachers.

The other teacher was a lifeguard. Rosie was lucky enough to find one at a public pool who took the time to call out instructions. Most pools now have lifeguards who are qualified to teach. Many of them know the new strokes and won't mind giving occasional pointers. Even with goggles, you can't see what you're doing as well as another good swimmer can.

Swimming Like a Flying Fish
(Pull, don't push.)

Try this only if you are already a pretty good swimmer, and have someone standing by to help. Stay in the shallow end of the pool, if possible.

Tie a towel around your ankles to keep yourself from kicking and to add drag.

Now swim the crawl. You will quickly find that, in order not to sink, you've got to start *pulling*. Pulling *feels* different.

After doing a lap or two, untie the towel. Add a slow kick, but continue to pull as before. Work on strengthening and streamlining the motion. After a few months of practice you may get that "flying fish" feeling. That makes it all worthwhile.

Pulling works better than pushing. The old flutter kick was supposed to push you from behind. Studies have proved that all it really does is to keep you balanced and floating. That's why, with the towel around your legs, you sink, until you really start to pull with your arms.

Pull Patterns

You can practice streamlined strokes out of the water. Every swimmer develops their own style of pulling. What the styles should have in common is that arms and hands are kept close to the body during the pull.

The old windmill strokes push you down in the water, more than pulling you forward.

And it's the same with flutter kicking. New swimmers kick like scuba divers: legs straight, movement slow and shallow, just under the surface.

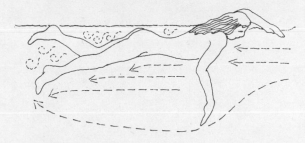

Look Below

Goggles have another use besides helping you see your strokes. They can do for swimmers what masks do for skin divers: they open up the underwater world. Even a concrete pool can be beautiful underwater. Swimmers move like dancers and the shimmering light makes even cement look soft.

In this world, the mind shuts down and the body takes over. It is easy to let your imagination roam. Call on it to help you swim better. Pretend you are swimming in tapioca pudding.

Imagine that your body is covered with cork. Or pretend you are an inflatable person, all hollow and full of air.

Swimming and running are excellent aerobic activities. Both can also be tiresome and boring. To get past monotony in running, you vary the pace and use your imagination as a helper. In new swimming, the same principles apply: vary the strokes, watch your own progress, get comfortable and enjoy the experience. These are all ways to make a good exercise fun.

An Amateur in the Big Swim

"**I** HAVE been swimming all my life, and I love it. But I've never done it competitively. My high school didn't have a swimming pool, and when I was younger it was sometimes hard to scare up a place to swim. In my teens there was a pool in my neighborhood — so I've just always been swimming, but I have never, like most of the other women in the Golden Gate swim, done any competitive swimming or even taken a lesson."

RACHEL THOMPSON is 29 years old and weighs 110 pounds. The picture was taken last fall after she had completed the third annual Women's Golden Gate Swim.

Marin County

Lime Rock
Alcatraz
G.G. Bridge
Fort Point

Route of the Swim

San Francisco

"**M**EN have been doing this for a long time, usually from the San Francisco side to the Marin County side. But we went from Lime Rock, on the Marin side, which is sort of right under the Golden Gate Bridge, to the beach right around the corner from Fort Point.

"**I**T'S a distance of about a mile and a quarter, which is not all that far. The problems, of course, are the tides and the temperature. The water can get to be ferociously choppy there, and the tides are very strong. The water temperature is usually in the low fifties.

"**T**IMING of the event is really important. There's a period of about

102

one-half hour when the tide is not going in either direction. It's actually harder for the slower swimmers. Like me: I came in next to last. I was in the water for 45 minutes, so in the last 15 minutes the tide was coming up and I had to swim harder to get to the beach than the better swimmers who made it in half an hour.

"THE rule, the theory about temperature, is that the people with more flesh on their bones are less bothered by the cold. For some reason, the cold doesn't bother me, and I'm one of the skinnier ones.

"IT was really difficult the first year. Not all the women made it. My friend Lane passed out, in the water, and didn't revive until she was back in the clubhouse. She would have drowned if someone hadn't seen her. But she entered again, the second year, and she made it across.

"THIS year there were 34 women. Everyone made it across. The woman who came in first did it in 25 minutes. There were some who were out for records. Then there were people like me who just wanted to make it across. That's the greatest victory for me, just finishing.

"ALL the swimmers were thrilled that everybody made it. Everybody cheered for the person who was first and said 'Wonderful, you made it first.' And everybody cheered just as much for the person who was last and said 'Great, we're really glad you made it.'

"FOR a person like me who's naturally high-strung and intense, one of my greatest enemies is tension. Tension and nervousness prevent me from being able to succeed in lots of things, but particularly physical things. If it's a mental battle, I'm used to that. But I'm not used to overcoming tension in physical things.

"THEN just a few years ago I discovered something: You do the best you can — period. That sounds very simple and dumb, but I realized it first in my work — that I was able to take risks, to do something on my own and know that if I failed, it was my own fault. At the same time, that freed me up to take risks physically. I don't think I've gotten past thinking of things in terms of success or failure, but I've made a big step toward accepting myself as I am: a not especially physically talented person, but someone who loves being outside, and who loves being active. I know what winning is for me. And I know now that I can do it."

12

Handmade Sports

Have you ever built a soapbox racer or "scrammy"? If you have, you can probably recall the excitement of your first ride in something you built with your own hands. New Games hold that same kind of excitement when you design and make your own equipment. Imagine the fun of seeing other people having a good time with something that you made.

Many New Games use no equipment at all other than human bodies. Some use standard balls and sporting equipment in new ways. Another type of New Game uses equipment that was never intended for sports, and a fourth type uses equipment specially designed for the game. It's these last two types that are the subject of this chapter.

Equipment You Can Make

First, think about your own physical fitness needs. If you live where winters keep you indoors a lot, you might want to build an indoor family gym. Start small and add equipment as you find the time and interest.

WEIGHT TRAINING MADE CONCRETE

Coffee cans and concrete are a tried-and-true way of making inexpensive dumb-bells and barbells. Here are some simple designs:

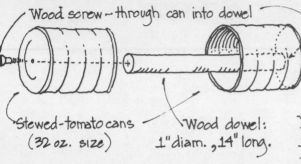

Wood screw – through can into dowel

Stewed-tomato cans
(32 oz. size)

Wood dowel:
1" diam., 14" long.

The cans, plus the dowel, will weigh about 12 ounces. So to make a 5-pound dumbbell, put 34 ounces of concrete in each can:

$$(12 + 34 + 34 = 80 \text{ oz.} = 5 \text{ lb.})$$

You can measure and mix the concrete a little at a time. Measure it (dry) with a mail scale. It will weigh the same before it's mixed with water as it will after it sets.

Use Ready-Mix concrete (the kind with sand and gravel already in it). A 90 lb. bag costs a little over $2.00. One bag will make a lot more weights than you can use, but that's the smallest size you can usually get. Follow directions on the bag carefully.

WARNING: Concrete contains cement, which is CAUSTIC. That means it can burn! Avoid contact by wearing gloves and goggles. Wash promptly after handling. If any mix gets in eyes, flush them with water repeatedly and call a doctor.

A Frisbee makes an excellent flexible mold for casting barbell weights. Here's how:

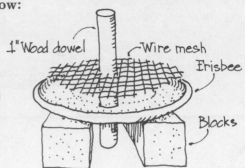

1" Wood dowel — Wire mesh

Frisbee

Blocks

You may need some help drilling a 1-inch hole through the center of the Frisbee. Push the dowel through the hole and stand the Frisbee on a couple of wooden blocks so the dowel can extend through a bit.

Cut a circle of wire mesh (can be "hardware cloth", or fine mesh "poultry netting"). The wire mesh should fit over the dowel and just inside the Frisbee. Mix up 2 pounds of concrete. Pour this into the Frisbee. Put the wire mesh on top of this first layer. Now add 2 more pounds of concrete and tamp it all down to remove any air bubbles.

Put wet cloths over the mold (to keep the outside from setting faster than the inside). Wait for at least 2 days. Remove the mold carefully, (you can reuse it), and tap out the dowel. Now you have a fine 4-pound "bell". Make some more, and slide them onto a wooden dowel to make adjustable-weight bar bells:

BUNGY CORD EXERCISER

Flexible-cord exercisers are sold in department stores and on television for $7.95 and up. Why not make your own with "bungy cords"? These are the kind of stretchy cords sold in hardware stores for tying down tarps and for holding things on the tops of cars.

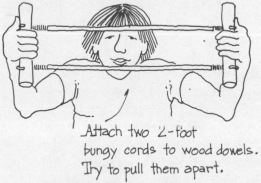

Attach two 2-foot bungy cords to wood dowels. Try to pull them apart.

Here's another cord exerciser you can make.

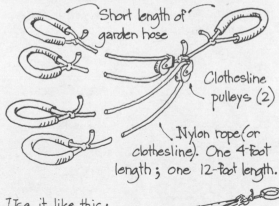

Short length of garden hose

Clothesline pulleys (2)

Nylon rope (or clothesline). One 4-foot length; one 12-foot length.

Use it like this:

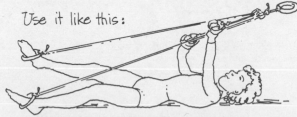

Hook one end to a bedpost or other sturdy support and slip your hands and feet into the four loops. Now lower your legs and arms in rhythm, working against the resistance of the clothesline. Remember to breathe normally.

Equipment Makes the Game

BALLOONATIC

Balloons are a cheap piece of equipment, full of play possibilities. Water balloon bombardment with your friends is a natural for warm, high-energy days.

You can also blow up the balloons with air and have a balloon-popping race.

Five or six balloons inflated and tied to a long string can become a "dragon's tail." Slay the "dragon" by trouncing all your partner's balloons (but watch out for your own).

A variation of this can be played on bicycles. (See chapter 13.)

ROPE TRICKS

Do you see any game possibilities in a 20-foot rope tied in a loop? No? Then you've obviously never played Giant Cat's Cradle. Remember the game you play with a loop of string on your fingers? Well, when the loop is 20 feet around, you can use people instead of fingers.

The same loop can be used for three-, four-, five-, or six-way tug-of-war. Space people around the loop. Extra players hang on to the waist of the player in front who is holding the waist of the player who's holding the rope. You can all pull in your own direction or gang up on the other teams.

SPIDER AND THE FLIES

(A game of tag, with strings attached.)

Each of at least four players gets a ball of kite string. The ends of all the strings are tied around a tree or post which be-comes the goal or center of the web. One player is the "spider." The spider covers its eyes and counts. The "flies" take off, leaving trails of string. When finished counting, the spider can advance along any string, looking for a fly. Each fly can hide, double back or join up with another fly. But wherever the flies go they must either leave a trail of string or follow a string trail made by another fly. The spider can catch a fly either by tagging or by seeing one.

What other games could you invent using balls of kite string?

CABLE SPOOL DERBY

Empty cable spools can sometimes be obtained free from telephone or power companies. Medium-size spools, when turned on their edges, make dandy two-wheeled chariots.

You could stage a race between two or three people of about the same size. Make sure the ground is pretty smooth, and keep the very little kids out of the way.

What other games can you invent with cable spools?

TUBE RACE

Get old inner tubes from a company that sells truck tires. (Car tires are mostly tubeless these days.) Stage a tube race by having contestants sit on the tubes and try to make them move. Touching the ground directly with feet or hands is not allowed.

What else could you play with inner tubes?

SUPER SLIDE

Get a 10-by-20-foot sheet of plastic from a hardware or builder's supply store (about $4.50). Unroll it on the ground, flood it with water from a garden hose, and you've got a dandy Super Slide.

MORE

Here are some other items that seem to beg to be a part of a New Game:

garden hose (attached to water supply or not)

old bedsheet

bale of hay

soap bubbles

plant sprayers (water only, please)

Have fun.

13

21 More New Games

Here are rules and equipment needs for 21 New Games, for two to two hundred people.

Hand Games

The simplest of all games begins with a handshake. When you greet and extend your hand to someone, you can also play a game. It's a great way to get to know people.

AMBITHUMBEROUS

Ever tried to thumb-wrestle with *both* hands? Any even number of people, two, four, six, etc., can do it. Some players will need to cross their arms.

Clasp hands like this:

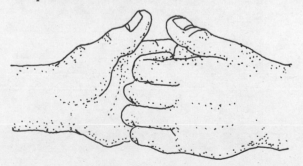

As in traditional thumb-wrestling, the object is to pin the other player's thumb beneath yours. But watch out for your other hand! Best strategy is to keep your eyes straight ahead, relying on your peripheral vision, and your *sense* of what your thumbs are doing.

UNRAVELLING

A group of 10 to 20 people is ideal for this game. (Larger numbers can be subdivided into groups of this size.)

The group gathers together in a tight circle, arms outstretched. In the sea of available hands, each person finds two to grasp. (Check to be sure the hands belong to two different people.)

Now, without letting go, try to unravel the chain into a big circle. Players may duck under the chain or step over it. The group is also allowed one application of

"knot-aid" — a quick letting go and hooking up again — to deal with an especially bad tangle.

The results will surprise you. Sometimes you get one big circle; sometimes a figure eight; sometimes two, three, or more independent circles. Some people will end up facing into the circle, some people facing out.

HUMAN PYRAMIDS

Three people can make a pyramid. So can six, and (maybe) ten. There are no rules for this game, but experience shows that you put your beefiest players on the bottom, the smallest on top. No knees directly over spines, please!

112

PRUIE? PRUIE!

A group of ten or more people gathers together in a loose array. A referee explains the rules: The object of the game is to find the "Pruie" (pronounced "proo-EE"). To do this you first close your eyes. (When everyone's eyes are closed, the referee picks someone to be the beginning of the Pruie.) Then everyone begins to mill around. If you touch someone, reach out, shake their hand, and ask them the question: "Pruie?"

If your answer comes back "Pruie!," then you have *not* found the Pruie. If you receive no answer at all, but the person continues to hold your hand, then you have found the Pruie. Congratulations!

When you find the Pruie, you become part of the Corporate Pruie, and you stay where you are. If someone shakes your free hand, do not reply, but continue to hold on to their hand. When everyone is part of the Pruie, the referee calls for everyone to open their eyes.

(Thanks to Bernie De Koven.)

SNAKE IN THE GRASS

This game was brought to the first New Games Tournament by a ten-year-old boy. Any number can play.

To start, the player who's "it" lies down in the grass and "becomes" a snake. All other players must make contact with the snake. At a signal (can be given by the snake or a referee) everyone jumps back trying not to be touched by the snake. Anyone touched becomes a snake too. The game continues until everyone is a snake.

WHO'S IN CHARGE?

A group of 5 to 20 people forms a circle and chooses a referee. One person volunteers to be "it." "It" stands in the center of the circle, with eyes closed, while the referee picks someone in the circle to be the leader.

The leader starts a repetitive movement, clapping hands, thumbing a nose, marching in place, etc., which everyone else in the circle must follow. "It" opens his or her eyes, and tries to determine who is leading the group. The leader must change the movement regularly, but always when "it's" back is turned, so as not to be caught in the act of changing.

To make the game more challenging, players should avoid looking directly at the leader.

When "it" either names the leader, or uses up three guesses, the leader becomes "it" for the next game, and takes a place in the center of the circle.

HUG TAG

This can be played with any number of people. The simple rules are: Any group of two players hugging (or holding hands) are a "free zone," and cannot be tagged. Players may start and stop hugging each other whenever they want.

The person who's "it" can hug people too. But you're still "it" until you find somebody who's unhugged and tag them.

(Thanks to Larry Diamond.)

STAND-OFF

Two players face each other at arm's length. (Use the shorter person's arms for the measurement.)

The feet of each player must be side by side, toes and heels touching.

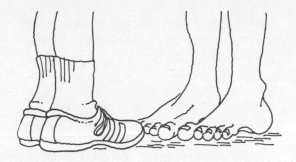

Players stand with knees and elbows slightly bent. Palms are toward the opposing player, about shoulder-width apart. The object of the game is to strike the other player's palms with yours. You score a point if you can push your partner off balance, causing them to move either foot. You, of course, must remain standing. You may also score by dodging one of your partner's thrusts, so that they lose balance and fall forward onto you. All kinds of faking and feinting movements are allowed.

One point is a game. The match is won by the player who takes two out of three games.

Note: The winner of a match may beat his or her chest and roar like a gorilla. (But this is optional.)

(Thanks to Scott Beach, Intergalactic Champion of Stand-Off.)

ROLL OVER, BEETHOVEN

This is a funny game that allows people to get very close together.

Any number can begin this game by simply lying, face down, on the ground. Scrunch together as tight as possible so there are no gaps; get to know your neighbors. Play begins with the person on one end of the line rolling over everybody to get to the other end. The game continues at least until everybody has had one roll.

THE HUMAN CENTIPEDE

This game needs at least 30 people. Players stand close together in a line that's three people wide, and ten or more people long. Players must not be shy; this is like a crowd in a subway — really packed in tight. A few other players, "side coaches," should stand at either side of the group to help keep it bunched together.

Play begins when one of the first people in the line is hoisted up onto the hands of the group, and passed, in a horizontal position, to the back of the line. When that person has been let down, and is in line again, another is passed from front to back. As play goes on, the whole group moves slowly backward like a giant centipede.

Side coaches should be ready to push back on "passengers" who get too close to the edges of the centipede.

YOGI TAG (DHO-DHO-DHO)

Any number can play this game, the ideal being from 10 to 20 people.

You'll need a fairly flat area, clear of brush and trees, within a space of at least 30 by 50 feet. The surface should be soft enough to cushion a fall: beach sand is ideal; soft grass is okay; you can even play indoors with tumbling mats.

Divide the playing field into two parts with a center line. This can be simply

a rope stretched across the ground, a line drawn in the sand, or a slight open space between the tumbling mats.

Players divide themselves evenly into two teams. A fair way to do this is to ask for birthdates: odd-numbered dates play on one side, evens on the other. Check to see that each team has the same number of players and even up any differences.

To play, the teams take turns sending one player across the center line. A flip of a coin can decide which team starts.

Now here's the catch: Before crossing the line, the player must take a deep breath, because for the whole time the player is in opposing territory, he or she must continually chant the non-sense words *dho-dho-dho . . .* without taking a breath. (*Dho* is pronounced as in cookie *dough*.) If the player (the "*dho-dho*") stops chanting at any time while on the other team's side, he or she must join the other team.

While on the other side, the *dho-dho* attempts to tag one or more players of the opposing team and return safely (still saying *dho-dho-dho*) to the home team. If the *dho-dho* can get any part of his or her body, even one finger, across the line before running out of breath, all the people who were tagged must switch sides.

Meanwhile, the opposing team is not just standing there waiting to be tagged. Their job is to grab the *dho-dho* and hold on until he or she runs out of breath. If they succeed, the *dho-dho* joins their team, and anyone the *dho-dho* may have tagged is free to stay on their original team.

As soon as one such interchange is complete, and the players, if any, have changed sides, the other team may send over a *dho-dho*. Your team can surprise the opposing team by sending over a *dho-dho* when they aren't paying attention.

Note: When capturing a *dho-dho*, do it as gently as possible. No running tackles; no holding below the waist. Anyone using unnecessary force must leave the game. A referee is useful to make sure everyone follows the rules.

(Thanks to George Leonard.)

Games with Equipment

You'll need to gather some supplies before you can put together the following games. For that reason, they are better suited to larger-scale, organized New Gaming, where many people can share the same equipment.

INFINITY VOLLEYBALL

As in regular volleyball, you'll need a net, a ball, and a level play area. Many of the rules of regulation volleyball apply, with these changes: Any number, from three to ten players, can make up a team. The two teams don't compete, they *cooperate* to get the highest score.

Scoring can work either of two ways: a point is scored each time the ball is hit; or each time it goes over the net. As in regular volleyball, there is a limit of three hits on one side of the net.

Everyone on both teams keeps score. Part of the fun is chanting the rising score together.

REVOLVING VOLLEYBALL

This is another variation on traditional volleyball. Rules for scoring remain the same. The difference is that after each point is scored, one member of each team changes sides. The make-up of a team is constantly changing, and it's never "us" against "them."

BOFFING

Here is a gentler version of the ancient art of saber fencing.

A point is taken for every loud "thwock" that the Styrofoam sword makes on your

117

partner's body. This is a great way to "let off steam" with nobody hurt.

Boffers sell for $14.00. This includes two Styrofoam swords with molded-in handles, two pairs of eye-and-ear guards, and postage. Order from:

New Games Foundation
P.O. Box 7901
San Francisco, California 94120.

LE MANS TUG-O-WAR

You'll need a sturdy rope 30 to 100 feet long. The more players, the longer and fatter the rope you'll need. For an all-out, 50-to-the-side event like the one shown here, better get a ship's hawser. A hawser is a 1- to 1½-inch diameter rope available at some surplus stores.

The *Le Mans start* originated in auto racing. At the starting gun, drivers had to run across the track, get in their cars, start them up, and roar off.

In Le Mans Tug-O-War, the rope is laid across a center line, or a water obstacle like a creek or sprinkler hose for added thrills. At the start, the two teams are on opposite sides of the center line, and no one is touching the rope. On a signal, each team runs to the *other* side of the line, picks up the rope, and begins pulling.

Grunts, yells, organized "heave-hos," and all other manner of vocalizations are encouraged. If one side is losing ground badly, it is considered good sportsmanship for some players from the stronger side to come to the aid of the weaker.

118

PARACHUTE MADNESS

While searching through your local surplus stores for a ship's hawser, keep an eye peeled for a used parachute. There are lots of them around, so you can afford to be selective. Check to be sure the parachute is a flat one. Nylon chutes are best because they're light. There's a whole range of sizes and colors, and the prices vary widely, from $15.00 to $60.00 or more. But a parachute will last a long time. If you do get a tear, patch it right away, before the tear becomes a gash. You can make a temporary repair with tape and then sew it up when you have time.

Parachutes, like balls, are natural playthings, full of possibilities for all kinds of games. Here are just a few to get you started:

Put as many people as you can comfortably fit around the edge of the parachute. Everyone grabs on to the edge, and lifts it into the air.

Now throw an Earth Ball (see below), or several big beach balls onto the parachute.

to keep the balls rolling around on the parachute. Balls that start to go out can be batted back in with hands and arms.

Another game is to have everybody grab the edge of the chute, quickly raise it up in the air, and, *while still holding the edge*, run under it. Quickly sit down on the edge as the chute settles down on your heads. Now lean back against the taut fabric and begin to sway your bodies back and forth. The parachute will take up an absolutely eerie movement.

Cooperate to pull the chute so as to make "waves." The idea is to work together

Parachutes are also fun to run under and over.

BICYCLE GYMKHANA

The word "gymkhana" comes from India by way of England, where it is used to describe an unusual kind of automobile race. Competition is against the clock, and a variety of driving skills are necessary to qualify with the best time. Here is a gymkhana adapted for bicycles. True to the tradition, speed alone will not give the best time. Instead, a mixture of good balance, accuracy, practice, and a well-maintained bike should carry the day.

HOW TO PLAY:

This course is only a suggestion. Use it to get started, but by all means, add your own inventions.

Lay out a course on a little-used street, parking lot, or other paved area. Chalk, sticks, small stones, tin cans, even poured sand can all be used to mark the course.

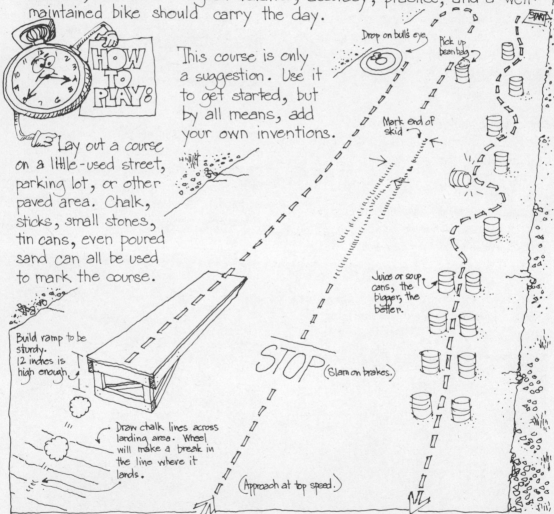

Drop on bull's eye

Pick up bean bag

START

Mark end of skid

Juice or soup cans, the bigger, the better.

Build ramp to be sturdy. 12 inches is high enough.

Draw chalk lines across landing area. Wheel will make a break in the line where it lands.

STOP (Slam on brakes.)

(Approach at top speed.)

The "winner" is the player who completes the course in the least time... BUT for each can knocked over <u>add</u> 5 seconds. For the shortest stopping time <u>subtract</u> 10 seconds. For the longest jump <u>subtract</u> 10 seconds.

The Bicycle in Joust

With just a little imagination, the modest bicycle becomes a mighty steed, the neighborhood street becomes a medieval amphitheater:

BALLOON-TAIL

This game is made doubly exciting by the fact that you cannot plan an offense without also being on the defense. As soon as you move in to quash your opponent's balloon-tail, your own becomes horribly vulnerable! Start by tying 5 or 6 balloons to an 8-foot length of light string (if it's light, it won't do any damage when it gets tangled in the spokes). Tie the balloon string to the back of your bike, leaving enough slack so that this balloon reaches the ground when the bike is not moving. Now adjust your armor and mount up. (Crash helmets are not a bad idea to prevent head injuries in falls.) Last rider with an unpopped balloon is not a rotten egg.

BAG TAG

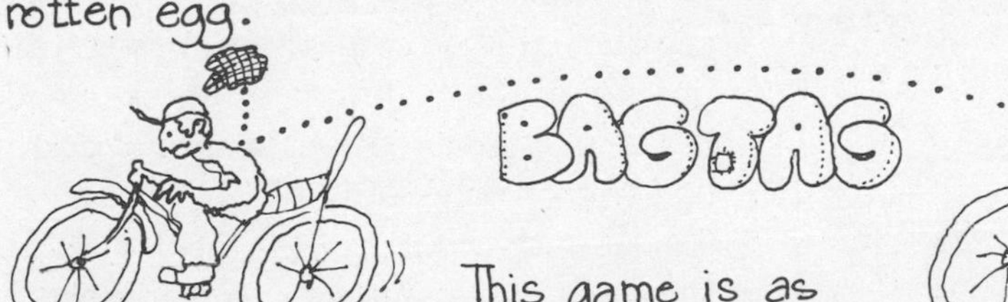

This game is as simple as its name. The 'it' person, while riding a bike, tries to throw and hit another rider with a bean bag. (A wet sponge will do as well.) Part of the fun is trying to pick up the bag or sponge without stopping. Less strict rules allow you to stop your bike to get it.

EARTH BALL

Earth Ball has become a kind of trade-mark for New Games. It's a spectacular game, full of large, sweeping movement that seems to capture everyone's imagination.

An official New Games Earth Ball, with silk-screened tan continents on blue oceans, is available from:

New Games Foundation
P.O. Box 7901
San Francisco, California 94120

The cost is about $250.00. An unpainted Earth Ball is about $200. (Write for exact prices, specifications, and delivery times.)

That rather steep cost is offset somewhat by the pageantry that an Earth Ball game brings to any New Games Festival. It is also one game that almost everyone will try. (See chapter 14 for ideas on how to raise money for an Earth Ball.)

To play, teams can divide themselves by birthdates, odds against evens. The most spectacular start comes from having teams line up on the goal lines at opposite ends of the play area. The field should be level and free of holes and brush. The ball is placed in the center of the field, and, at the starting signal, teams converge on the ball with appropriate yells and screams.

The object of the game is to move the ball across the other team's goal line. In actual play, scoring goals is uncommon. The fun is in feeling the team power, and moving the Earth, especially when it's up and bouncing along on a hundred hands. In their enthusiasm, often players even forget what side they're on, but no one seems to notice.

ORBIT

This is a space-saving Earth Ball game played in two concentric circles.

The inside circle of people lies on their backs, heads toward the center. The other players stand, facing inward to make the outside circle. When the ball is put into play, the inside team tries to kick the ball over the heads of the outside team. The outside team must keep the ball within their circle and in the air at all times.

It's important to remember that because New Games are new, there are no experts. Another way to look at it is that *everyone's* an expert.

Make use of the enthusiasm that exploring something new can turn on in poeple. Use it to invent more New Games.

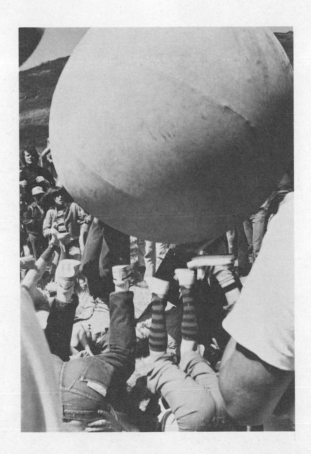

A Real New Games Festival

THIS Festival took place on the Triple range of a partly abandoned Army base. Seeing people play and let off steam harmlessly makes you stop and think: Will New Games someday replace military games?

THERE were three volleyball nets with action all day long. There were Earth Ball games, Tug-O-Wars, Parachute Madness, New Frisbee and Bopping. There was also a game called Tweezly Wop:

TWEEZLY WOP is kind of like a pillow fight on a log horse. The pillows are burlap sacks partly filled with straw. More straw under the horse cushions the inevitable fall.

LAP SITTING is maybe the ultimate game of cooperation. First you make a huge circle standing shoulder-to-shoulder. Then you all turn to the right and sit down on the lap of the person behind you. At the same time you make a lap for the person in front. Here's how it looks, before...

...and after:

THE World Record for Lap Sitting is now somewhere over a thousand people. Care to try for more?

FACE PAINTING is something that even the youngest games players will try. All that's needed is poster paint and brushes:

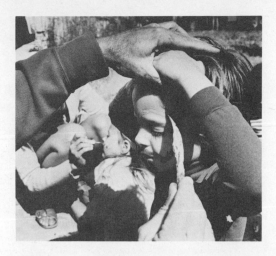

GETTING this many people together carries some responsibilities. The Red Cross was on hand just in case. But the only emergency turned out to be a shortage of toilet paper:

HUNGER is not a New Game. But here's a portable approach to filling the need:

WHEN people are encouraged to be inventive and playful, you get some nice surprises: The game was one-legged soccer. (You tie one of your legs to a partner's with a belt or scarf, and play that way.) The problem was to make boundaries. Since everyone was removing their shoes to make the game safer, someone got the idea of using the shoes for lines:

14

New Games Festival

Can you imagine your friends, your family, your whole neighborhood playing New Games? It's a great way to bring people together, and New Games are exciting, even fun, to organize. The trick is to start small. Think of your first venture as an experiment. Let your New Games Festival grow naturally and learn to organize by doing. Make it bigger and better each time.

There are a few tried and tested ideas about New Games, and they apply to gatherings of from ten to ten thousand people. No matter how big your event becomes, keep these "big ideas" in mind and your organizing will be smoother.

Big Ideas

Setting the stage: New Games are noncompetitive in spirit. Likewise, the organization of a New Games Festival should not compete with the games themselves. The most successful approach is to set the stage: make sure all the gaming equipment, decorations, food, clean-up and sanitation needs, etc., are *there*. Then join in the games yourself. The best kind of organization becomes invisible on the day of the event.

A game for everybody: From kite-flying on a grassy slope, to little kids painting their faces, to Le Mans Tug-O-War, New Games Festivals provide something for everybody. There should be an activity for every size, age, and kind of person.

Something always happening: A core of organized, regularly scheduled games can take up the slack from the more casual, free-form events. The idea is to have some games planned down to the minute. (Then be prepared to abandon the plan!)

No spectators: A New Games Festival is a party where everyone is both host *and* guest. Give everyone the responsibility for cleaning, policing, refereeing. There are no experts in New Games.

Good communications: Since you'll want to plan for flexibility, you'll need a means for keeping everyone aware of the changes. Signs, flags, megaphones, are all ways to stay in touch.

Food and cleanup: New Games take lots of human energy, which has to be renewed with food and drink. If you're organizing, you can plan to provide it yourself, or ask people to bring their own, or both. Food creates garbage, but cleaning up can be turned into a game too.

Human needs: New Games means nobody hurt, hopefully. But be prepared with first aid just in case. Humans also need water, sanitation, a lost and found; depending on the scale of your New Games Festival, you may have to help supply these needs for your group.

Festivities: New Games can be beautiful. An ideal location, perfect weather — these you can only hope for. But flags, banners, balloons, and other decorations can raise spirits, even on cloudy days.

Getting the Ball Rolling

Where: The first New Games Festival was held in a beautiful, open valley near the Pacific Ocean, just eight miles from San Francisco. The site was perfect. There was a creek which became the center obstacle for Tug-O-War. There were grassy slopes from which to fly kites. There were open fields for giant games of Earth Ball. And there was an abundance of warm California sun.

A later New Games Festival was held in a mini-park in the heart of a big city.

There has also been a successful New Games Festival in a warehouse on a cold November night.

In other words, a beautiful location is nice, but not necessary.

Picking a site: New Games can be played in a vacant lot, in a city park, or indoors in a gymnasium. Instead of the game dictating the space needed, let the space available help dictate the way the games are played. Basketball played on a 20-by 20-foot court becomes an entirely different game. An Earth Ball game can take up a whole football field. But it is equally challenging in a 30-foot circle.

As you look over possible sites, imagine playing the games there. A volleyball net here, Bicycle Gymkhana there, and so on.

What and when: Okay, you've decided on a site. Next you'll need to set a date for the event and go about announcing it. Word-of-mouth is the best, because you can talk to people and find out what questions they have. You can also print some posters and distribute them.

You can tack these to telephone poles, or deliver them door-to-door, or slip them under windshield wipers.

Another way to promote the event, and also get some volunteer help, is to stage a *mini-festival.* Just plant yourself and a friend or two in a spot where people in your neighborhood congregate. It could be outside the supermarket on Saturday, in a park, or in front of the school or church. (Things will be smoother if you

check in with the powers-that-be in these places just to tell them what you're doing.)

At the mini-festival you can demonstrate a New Game or two by playing them. (Stand-Off and Boffing are good because they're exciting, two-people games that don't take a lot of space.) You can also talk about the New Games ideas and pass out posters. You could set up a card table with a notebook where people can sign up to help. Make sure you get the message across: New Games are for everybody. Even adults.

For equipment, printing, and other pre-Games expenses, approach local merchants. To be more persuasive, you can offer to make a sign which will announce the merchants' donations at the Festival.

It's usually easier to get hold of goods rather than cash. You might approach a sporting goods store for a donation of game equipment. Ask a printer to contribute paper and printing services. Ask a grocer for food prizes. (Watermelons for an eating contest can be a big hit in the summer.)

As Games day approaches, you'll want to think about these other preparations:

Check the site for possible hazards, like broken glass and potholes. Hard-packed earth, or paved areas can be cushioned by spreading a few bales of straw (donated).

Set up tables for the sale of food and drink, and/or picnic tables where people can eat their picnic lunches. (Tables can be borrowed for the day from a church, school, or club.)

Have a training session for volunteer referees. Teach by example. Let the referees learn by actually playing a game you organize.

Make arrangements for first aid, drinking water, and sanitation. If your event is for less than 50 or so people, you can ask someone who lives near the site to let people use the facilities in their home. If there are public toilets nearby, in a school, church, etc., arrange to use those.

Decorate the grounds. Paint signs and murals on brown wrapping paper, for instance. Make flags with poster paint on muslin. Balloons are inexpensive and festive. So is crepe paper. Kites are colorful, either in the air or hanging on fences.

Saturday afternoons seem to be good times for New Games. Try not to schedule your event in competition with weddings, birthday parties, or other holiday happenings. On the other hand, Memorial Day, Labor Day, and Fourth of July weekends are naturals for a New Games Festival.

After the games are over, you can make a game out of cleaning up. Give a prize for the biggest collection of paper cups, the most gum wrappers, and so on. Or have everybody form a line across one end of the site. Give each person a paper or plastic bag and have them move in a line from one end of the site to the other, like locusts, devouring every piece of litter in their path.

Very likely your first New Games Festival will make you a believer. Then you may want to hold another one, only bigger and better. Here are some ideas for expanding a New Games Festival.

A Bigger Site

Getting permission: Parks, beaches, and recreation areas are all excellent choices for large-scale New Games Festivals, as long as they are close to urban areas. When you come upon a likely site, find out who maintains the property: U.S. Government, state, county, or city. Write or call the recreation director, or public information person in that agency and describe what you want to do.

More than likely you will be warmly received. Most of these directors are looking for new ways to involve people in outdoor recreation. In addition, New Games have been given lots of positive attention in the media. They have been recognized as a good way to bring all kinds of people together for non-destructive use of recreation lands.

If you need help convincing an agency to give permission, you can write to:

New Games Foundation
P.O. Box 7901
San Francisco, California 94120

They can send you information about past successes and lists of agencies that have proved to be enthusiastic about New Games.

Getting sponsored: All of your organizational efforts may go more smoothly if you find a *sponsor.* If you can tie up with a local group that is a recognized, public-spirited organization, their reputation may rub off on you. Caution: This can also backfire. Don't let a sponsor apply too much pressure and wreck the spontaneity of your event. Tell them that New Games

are *new*, and therefore something of an experiment. Tell them you need lots of support, and also lots of room in which to let your "baby" grow.

Likely sponsors are:

Churches (try the young people's groups).

Schools (try the PTA, booster clubs, even the athletic departments).

Police or fire departments (they often have groups within their departments that help organize community projects).

Fraternal organizations (try the Lions Club, Odd Fellows, Eastern Star, Rotary, Junior Chamber of Commerce, etc.).

Scouting organizations (Girl and Boy Scouts, Campfire Girls, etc.).

Neighborhood associations (La Familia, Hadassah, etc.).

Big Brothers, Big Sisters.

Social service agencies (single parents' groups, family service agencies, etc.).

Conservation groups (National Audubon Society, local chapters of the Sierra Club, Nature Conservancy, etc.).

Sponsors can help you get permission to use property. (Or they may already own a site that is usable.) They can also help you through the maze of getting insurance coverage; with luck, your event can be covered under a policy the sponsors already have.

Sponsors may offer you office space, telephones, copying equipment, and supplies. They may also be helpful with publicity.

You may want to work with a sponsor in setting up food and drink concessions, dividing the expenses and income.

Getting people to help: Sponsors are also a good source of people who will want to join in organizing the Festival. Be firm and clear about the kind of help you need:

Artists (to draw posters, make signs, flags, and so on).

Copywriters (to write announcements, advertisements, radio spots, etc.).

Publicists (people to contact newspapers and radio stations to get free "plugs").

Someone with a relative in the insurance business (to help you with liability coverage).

Talent scout (someone to contact clowns, mimes, puppeteers, make-up artists, musicians, and other performers who may contribute their talents).

Food and drink organizer.

Cleanup organizer (should be someone with knowledge of recycling).

Land steward (works with the land owner making sure the site is properly cared for).

Human needs organizer (sanitation, first aid, water, lost and found, etc.).

Communications chief (responsible for on-site communications: signs, walkie-talkies, megaphones, emergency telephones).

Referee coach (teaches volunteer referees how to teach others to play games).

Transportation chief (looks into mass transit, car pools, etc., to and from the Games).

Spectacle chief (in charge of giving the Games a festive look).

Now you're in the big leagues. Are you having a good time organizing New Games? Good. You must be a natural organizer.

For some people, even something as free-wheeling as a New Games Festival can give them organizational nightmares. But don't forget: If it's grown this big, it can also grow small again. Go back to neighborhood New Games if that's more your speed. After all, remember the test for New Games? The last (but not least) question is: Is it fun?

Epilogue

There are sprinters.
And there are long-distance runners.

As far as New Games go, reading this book
is like finishing a short sprint.
There's a lot more to know, and to do.

Keep on running.
But keep it playful.

Going Further

Yoga for Beginners Alice K. Turner. A compact, well-illustrated guide to doing about a dozen asanas. Franklin Watts, Inc., New York, 1973.

Jump Rope Peter L. Skolnik. Jump rope rhymes, techniques, and fitness. Just about everything you could possibly want to know about jumping rope. Workman Publishing Co., New York, 1974.

Beyond Jogging Mike Spino. Running made natural. Varying the pace. Your imagination as a running partner. Celestial Arts, Millbrae, California, 1976.

Aikido in Daily Life Koichi Tohei. A guide to the practice of a gentle martial art by a warm and wise teacher. Rikugei Publishing House, Tokyo, Japan, 1966.

Chairman Mao's 4 Minute Physical Fitness Plan Maxwell L. Howell, D.Ph., Ed.D. Complete, illustrated instruction in all eight of Chairman Mao's exercises. Celestial Arts, Millbrae, California, 1973.

Athletic Fitness Dewey Schurman. The latest conditioning techniques from professional athletic trainers. Includes yoga-like stretching exercises, weight training and athletic diet. Well illustrated with photographs. Atheneum, New York, 1975.

Yoga Conditioning & Football Jerry Colletto with Jack L. Sloan, Ed.D. This high school team had won 40 straight games without a single injury. Their yoga training techniques are illustrated with photographs. Celestial Arts, Millbrae, California, 1975.

Rules of the Game The Diagram Group. "The Complete Illustrated Encyclopedia of all the Sports of the World." A very handsome book. Available in paperback. Paddington Press, New York, 1974.

The New Games Book Andrew Fluegelman, editor. A giant collection of New Games and how to play them. By the people who started it all, with help from their friends. Headlands Press/Doubleday, San Francisco, 1976.

Out of Their League Dave Meggyesy. An eye-opening personal account of what it's like to play football for a living. Ramparts Press, Inc., San Francisco, 1970.

The Ultimate Athlete George Leonard. This is not an easy book to read, but the chapter on New Physical Education is recommended for anyone who takes "p. e." in school. Viking Press, New York, 1975.

Acknowledgements:

Rules for Orbit, Le Mans Tug-O-War, Pruie, Hug Tag, Yogi Tag, Snake in the Grass, and Stand-Off adapted with permission from *The Whole Earth Ball* and other copyrighted publications of The New Games Foundation.

Photographs and portions of text from *Yoga Conditioning & Football* by Jerry Colletto. Copyright © 1975. Reprinted with permission of Celestial Arts, 231 Adrian Road, Millbrae, CA 94030, publisher.

"Basketball," an account of the invention of basketball reprinted with permission from *The Encyclopedia of Sports*, 5th ed., A. S. Barnes & Company, publisher. Copyright © 1975.

Photograph from *Athletic Fitness* by Dewey Schurman. Copyright © 1975. Reprinted by permission of Atheneum Publishers, New York.

Chart from *Aerobics* by Kenneth H. Cooper, M. D. Copyright © 1968. Reprinted by permission of M. Evans and Company, Inc., New York.

And thanks to:

ANDREW FLUEGELMAN, BURTON NAIDITCH, PAT FARRINGTON STEWART BRAND, et al., for inventing and nurturing the New Games idea, and for freely sharing the "wealth."

GEORGE LEONARD for writing *The Ultimate Athlete*.

LILLIE LEONARD for sending me off in new directions.

JAMIE JOBB for the library in his head.

BILL BRODER, and ADAM, for reading the manuscript and correcting my sports facts.

MIKE SPINO, ROSEMARY MENNINGER, and BILL MONTI for critiques and encouragement.

MARIE DERN and DOUG McCOY for research.

RACHEL THOMPSON for ideas and the photograph on page 133.

ROBERT FOOTHORAP for the photo of Rachel Thompson, page 102.

BRIAN GILBERT for the photograph on page 103.

RAY RAVAGLIA, and ERIC, for the photograph on page 89.

ROBERT PONCE for the photograph on page 72.

CURTIS, STACI, JOLIE, PHILIP, TANÉ, and JORDY for the cover.

MARILYN, MARTHA, JIM, DAVID, and LINDA for demonstrating that it could be done.

JIM for suggesting I do it.

DEBORAH for sustenance.

MOM and DAD for not pushing me into athletics. They let me come to it when I was ready — at age 34.